5871

RELIGIOUS

Rock 'n' Roll

A Wolf In Sheep's Clothing

BY JIMMY SWAGGART
with Robert Paul Lamb

Jimmy Swaggart Ministries
P.O. Box 2550
Baton Rouge, Louisiana 70821-2550

CONTENTS

Introduction

Chapter 1   New Year's Eve Madness   1

Chapter 2   The Origins Of Music   13

Chapter 3   Religious Rock 'n' Roll   27

Chapter 4   Music For Evangelism   45

Chapter 5   Mixing The Sacred And Sexy   57

Chapter 6   What's The Message?   69

Chapter 7   The Influence Factor   83

Chapter 8   Heavy Metal Missionaries 97

Chapter 9   The Superstars 107

Chapter 10   Religious Rock And The Church 123

Chapter 11   What's Ahead? 135

Chapter 12   Southern Gospel 143

Chapter 13   What To Look For In Christian Music   153

Chapter 14   Who Or What's To Blame? 163

Chapter 15   *Crossfire:* An Alternative 173

Afterword

INTRODUCTION

 om Brokaw, NBC News anchorman, closed his November 10, 1986, Evening News program with an item about rock and roll singer Bruce Springsteen's unprecedented five-record album release, *Bruce Springsteen & The E Street Band Live 1975-1985*.

According to Brokaw, more than 5 million copies of the album had been pressed with 1.5 million shipped to record stores "and most of those sold to frantic customers standing in long lines the first day at $30 each."

"Parents, teach your children to sing rock and roll," Brokaw said with a wry smile.

The fact that the release of a rock and roll album could command national news attention and bring in more revenues — perhaps $450 million — than any other album ever recorded tells you something of what has happened in this country since the rock music craze was introduced more than thirty years ago.

To some, it seems that disc jockey Alan Freed's words have become prophetic: "Anyone who says rock 'n' roll is a passing fad or a flash-in-the-pan trend along the music roads has rock in the head, Dad," said the man who coined the rock music term.

"Let's face it — rock 'n' roll is bigger than all of us," he predicted.

Over the years, it has not been difficult for discerning Christians to follow the alarming trends as rock music increasingly spewed death, drugs, and destruction across the land.

No reasonable, informed person — born again or otherwise — could seemingly ever question if this musical medium was not satanically inspired.

Who would have ever thought the influence of rock music would intrude into the Church of Jesus Christ and help spawn another musical form — religious rock and roll.

Yet it has happened.

James Chute of the *Milwaukee Journal* has correctly observed:

> Not accidentally, when contemporary music first moved into the Christian worship service almost two decades ago — marking the beginning of the CCM movement — it came in the form of folk music where the words so essential to worship could be understood over the music.
>
> The CCM movement, however, has gone far beyond a few musicians strumming guitars and singing in harmony . . .

For a number of years — actually dating back to July 1980 — I have been attempting to call the body of Christ's attention to an alarming trend which developed first as so-called contemporary Christian music.

Yet as I watched secular rock music grow in satanic intensity, subverting the minds and morals of young people in this nation, I have also witnessed a dramatic change in the early 1980s in the religious music realm.

Again, I wrote another article — "Christian Rock & Roll" — for our ministry publication, *The Evangelist,* in February 1985 about these disturbing trends in the body of Christ. I did so again in January 1987 with a story, "Rock 'n' Roll Music in the Church."

But as religious rock has grown into a multi-million dollar business — embraced by churches, Christian TV networks, radio stations, record companies, and magazines — subsequently affecting the lives of millions of believers, the time has come for something to be said beyond a periodic article.

That alone is the reason for this book.

Up front, I would like to say that I have nothing but Christian love and goodwill for every single individual involved in religious rock.

Although it has been necessary to name specific music artists in order to cite activities I find objectionable, worldly, and not promoting the cause of Christ, nothing in this book should be construed as labeling or accusing any musical group, song, or record album as being satanic.

My disagreement is not fundamentally with these people but with their music and methods which I believe are not in harmony with the Gospel of Jesus Christ. I am most disturbed at pastoral leadership which permits the foregoing under the guise of a tool of evangelism.

Ezekiel 44:23 gives this charge to God's priests:

> *"And they shall teach my people the difference between the holy and profane, and cause them to discern between the unclean and the clean."*

As an evangelist, that's one of my God-given responsibilities — to help people recognize what is clean and unclean, what is holy and unholy. And even though my voice is almost alone in addressing this subject, these things *must* be said.

This book comes after much prayer and months of research and review by myself and co-author, Robert Paul Lamb. Chapter One, "New Year's Eve Madness," represents Robert Paul's firsthand view of a Stryper concert in San Jose, California.

Some may not even want to look at this issue of religious rock because it has simply become an idol to them. Yet I encourage you to read this book very carefully. Hear what the religious rockers are saying . . . look at the spirit they are conveying . . . then hear what the Word of God says.

At that point, there can be little doubt your conclusion will be the same as ours: *Religious Rock and Roll, A Wolf in Sheep's Clothing.*

Jimmy Swaggart

CHAPTER
ONE

NEW YEAR'S EVE MADNESS

 tryper has had several concert cancellations . . . but we'll be in San Jose on New Year's Eve to set the record straight . . . And don't forget, 'To Hell with the Devil.' . . .

— Phone message from Stryper's Concert Hotline

December 31, 1986. New Year's Eve.

San Jose, California, about fifty miles south of San Francisco, is gray and overcast. The weather is cold, damp, 41 degrees. A wisp of misty rain is falling.

The lighted marquee above the beige-shaded, tile-roofed, Spanish-stucco Civic Auditorium on busy Market Street announces: "Stryper, Alcatrazz, 9 P.M."

Stryper's west coast tour has already been cut short with cancellations in two California cities, Redding and Sacramento. I was told poor ticket sales in Sacramento had caused that concert to be scrubbed, and I've driven over two hours from California's capital city to see religious rock's most controversial band in concert.

Two hours before the show, a small cluster of youngsters has gathered outside the auditorium's entrance. An hour later, a line is stretching from the main doors, down the sidewalk, and around the Market Street side of the building.

Beer cans and cigarettes are passed among some standing in line. The scent of marijuana wafts through the air. An empty six-pack of California Cooler (a white wine/citrus drink) litters the sidewalk. Several liquor bottles have been dumped among the evergreens and shrubbery around the structure.

Only some ten people or so are admitted into the auditorium where they are physically searched. "No cameras, no tape recorders, no drugs, no weapons" shouts a burly man at the door wearing a red Stryper T-shirt proclaiming "To Hell with the Devil" in black and yellow letters on the front. A card pinned to his shirt says "Stryper staff."

Several long-haired young men behind me are cursing over the line's slowness in the misty rain. Ticket scalpers call out: "Got your tickets?"

A long white limousine pulls up and disgorges three people after an extended wait — two men and a woman, all dressed in black. A few cars drop off teens not yet of driving age.

Instead of New Year's Eve, it somehow seems like a belated Halloween with the dizzying array of offbeat clothes worn by most of the concert-goers. Many are dressed in punk or new-wave attire — spiked or colored hair, oversized shirts, black leather knuckle gloves, spiked armbands, boots. A number of girls wear short, bright-colored skirts and heavy black eye makeup.

One thin young man dressed in black jeans, a black T-shirt and vest, black eye shadow, and sporting a cross earring, is forced to remove a set of metal chains and handcuffs wrapped around his waist. Several others are confronted at the door over their arm or wristbands of leather and metal.

Another boy, apparently in his late teens, is wearing thigh-high white leather boots with platform soles to match his spiked silver-blonde hair. He is refused temporary admission until he removes spiked wristbands.

Inside the auditorium's front corridor against a wall called the "Freedom Shrines," a brisk business in Stryper souvenirs — photos, buttons, posters, bumper stickers, and T-shirts — is under way on either side of the twin doors leading to the main floor.

One of the oddest sights of the evening comes when a Catholic priest dons a red Stryper T-shirt announcing "To Hell with the Devil" and pulls the garment over his clerical collar and shirt, then rolls up the sleeves revealing a tattooed cross on his left upper arm.

When asked about his actions, the priest identifies himself as pastor of a Bay area Catholic church who has brought two teenage boys from his youth group to the concert. "I don't own a TV set," he says, "but I have a radio and I prefer rock and roll."

The two teens don't buy a shirt, but many of the T-shirt purchasers are like the Catholic priest. They put on the shirt immediately. It's like a badge of identity.

Most of the crowd clearly are still in their teen years, although there seems to be a good number over twenty and beyond. Many are outfitted in skimpy black, form-fitting spandex or leather clothes, spiked or shoulder-length hair and garish colors.

Yet they stand alongside a sprinkling of curiosity-seeking kids you'd expect to sit beside in church — short hair, modest dress, and smiles.

By 8:30 p.m. the balcony has begun to fill with the noisy crowd. The area around the stage grows with several hundred of the early arrivals — many are smoking, talking, and milling around.

Recorded heavy metal rock music starts about 8:45 p.m. over the auditorium's sound system, the sound bouncing off the stucco walls and echoing throughout the building.

"Do you know the names of any of those groups playing?" I asked a pudgy girl who looked about sixteen standing alone.

"Yeah," she answered, almost disinterested. "They've played Aerosmith and Van Halen so far."

"How do you like it?" I wondered.

"Okay, I guess."

"How about Stryper? Do you know anything about their message?"

"Not really," she said with a shrug of her shoulders.

"Do you like their music?"

"Yeah."

"Why?"

"I don't like the devil, so I guess I like Stryper," she answered.

"Well, you must be a Christian then?" I smiled.

"No."

Six San Jose policemen, clad in crisp blue uniforms trimmed in white and gold and long black nightsticks, patrol the auditorium's circular corridors. One of the cops — a tall, muscular man with a thick mustache — talks freely with me, identifying himself as a Christian.

"Is this the only place in San Jose for rock concerts?" I asked.

"They've had them elsewhere but there were problems with the larger crowds at the Civic Center," he explained, "so they'll only permit this place to be used. It greatly restricts the turnout but it also limits the problems."

"What do you think about a rock group like Stryper that sings religious lyrics?"

His brow furrowed. "The sound and the message seem totally incompatible," he replied thoughtfully.

"Do you have teenagers?" I questioned.

"Yes — four girls."

"Would you let them come to a concert like this?"

"No," he said firmly, "and if they tried, I'd go as far as to lock them in their bedrooms."

At 9 o'clock, Alcatrazz, a five-man rock group from the San Francisco Bay area, hits the stage and rocks through 45 minutes of loud, ear-assaulting songs. The group's lead singer, a man with short hair wearing a sport jacket and slacks, stands out in sharp contrast to his band — most of which are wearing shoulder-length hair and surly looks.

None of the group's songs ever touch on a gospel theme or message. Their second number is fairly typical — a 1986 version of Eric Burdon and the Animals' hit from 1964 — "It's My Life . . . and I'll do what I want."

The song's lyrics seem to characterize what most everybody associated with this concert has in mind.

Two men in their mid-twenties, who identify themselves as being involved in a street ministry just getting started in San Jose, tell me they see Stryper speaking to a part of the culture the church is not reaching.

"The concert has been promoted entirely over rock stations in the area and has been handled by Bill Graham, the secular rock producer," reported the younger of the two men, dressed in black leather and wearing two earrings in his left ear.

"I'd say the kids here are about 80 percent from the world and about 20 percent Christian," he continued.

"What'll happen to these kids tonight?" I probed.

"Oh, they'll hear the Gospel — no question about that. That's the whole object . . . and we have tracts to give out. We'll be witnessing."

"Well, that's what I've come to hear," I said, "But I'm also interested in why they have a group like Alcatrazz on the show?"

"That's just to bring in more kids not connected to the church in any way . . . and I think it worked," the short, hyperactive man offered.

Walking around the downstairs waiting for Alcatrazz to finish its performance, I encounter four clean-cut teenage boys and a girl sitting on some steps to the balcony. They identify themselves as members of a church whose pastor is a prominent evangelical leader.

My question was obvious: "Why are you here?"

"I heard Stryper a couple years ago in L.A.," one boy answered. "They really impressed me then with their show and then going out into the audience to talk with people. I wanted to see what they are doing now."

"I've never seen them before," another teen told me. "That's why I came."

"Do you think they are really reaching anybody for the Lord?" I asked.

"We're not to judge," said a teenage boy with strong brown eyes. "That wouldn't be our place."

"I'm not talking about judging them," I explain. "I'm talking about discerning the difference between the holy and unholy. What about Jesus' words about false individuals coming in His name? What about the Bible's warning on conforming to the world's standards?"

"Some of *that* is so confusing," one of the boys says, a little bewildered. "Everybody has his point of view and sounds so right."

The crowd, which appears to have reached between 1,500 and 2,000 (nobody can give me a closer estimate), seems almost bored with the Alcatrazz group in spite of their loud, frantic sound and dancing antics on stage. Everybody has clearly come to see Stryper.

Finally, Alcatrazz has finished its depressing efforts and stagehands move at breakneck speed to clear away the equipment. A large sign proclaiming "To Hell with the Devil" in bright yellow and black letters dominates the backdrop.

The stage is now clothed in jet blackness. The house lights have also dimmed.

At 10:18 p.m., the eerie strands of Stryper's instrumental song "Abyss" begins rising through the sound system, imitating a trip into Dante's Inferno, evoking visions of the netherworld.

Immediately the crowd of several hundred standing in front of the stage erupts, chanting in unison: "Stryper, Stryper, Stryper."

In the balcony and throughout the main floor, cigarette lighters are lit and held high as some symbol of welcome while others are waving their right arms back and forth.

The ethereal sounds of "Abyss" — punctuated by the sound effects of moans, groans, and yelps — dominates the auditorium for what seems like an endless amount of time. Excitement builds . . . interest peaks . . . the air seems charged.

Then, gradually at first, then gaining speed, lights begin flashing on stage — first red, then blue, then yellow. Now — faster and faster and faster they flash.

Suddenly . . . CRASH . . . BAM . . . BOOM!!!

The stage ignites in a crescendo of lights, sights, and sounds. All four members of Stryper — Robert and Michael Sweet, Oz Fox, and Tim Gaines — are in place and roaring into the deafening sounds of their first song, "To Hell with the Devil."

The crowd, pressing against the stage, is screaming its approval; many are dancing. Hands clap; bodies boogie to the beat. Lights flash . . . red-blue-yellow. Spotlights blaze.

The three up-front musicians — Gaines, Fox, and Michael Sweet — are gesturing at the audience, shaking their heads of shoulder-length hair, dancing and strutting across the stage.

Drummer Robert Sweet, long blonde hair flying, flails away on drums inside a setting which looks something like a child's swing set which has been painted yellow and black.

The stage is dominated by the drum set and two run-ways leading to platforms on either side of the drummer's setting. Of course, everything is painted yellow and black as are the guitars, the drums, and the band's spandex-and-leather outfits.

The sound level is deafening almost beyond belief. The bone-crunching, ear-shattering, guitar-dominated music is exploding throughout the auditorium by the way of twenty speakers — ten each located on either side of the stage.

In the balcony, the words of the songs are indistinguishable. One of the street preachers has taken a seat nearby and I ask, "Can you understand any of these lyrics?"

"Not really," he smiles, "but you get used to it."

My policeman friend walks past on patrol. "Can you hear what the group is singing?" I asked.

"Nope."

From upstairs I have noticed four of Stryper's road crew standing between the stage and the first row of people pressing forward trying to reach the band. Occasionally an overzealous fan is pushed back from the stage.

After some twenty minutes in the balcony, I decide to get a closer view by going to the first floor. I want to see everything up closer — particularly one long-haired young man who has stripped off his leather vest and is dancing alone to the band's beat in the center of the floor.

Standing on the first floor gives an entirely different picture of the concert than in the balcony — yet most of the crowd is upstairs — maybe for safety's sake.

Fifty feet away from the stage itself, the floor is vibrating to the band's throbbing rhythm as Michael Sweet sings "rocking because you died for me." In fact, the beat seems to pulsate almost unbelievably at this range — my chest seems to be literally heaving from the sound. The sound is numbing.

After playing and dancing through three or four songs, lead singer Michael Sweet says to the crowd: "I see this is a rock and roll crowd tonight."

The crowd, especially those pressed against the front of the stage, shouts approval, and soon the group is blasting its way through another series of songs.

Steve Rabey's book, *The Heart of Rock and Roll,* did not sell Stryper short in describing the group's musical abilities:

> . . . These guys cook. We're not talking just simmer or medium warm here, but boiling, smoldering, power-driven rock.

Energetic and any related adjective in the book would describe Stryper's on-stage performance: vigorous, active, forceful, strenuous, dynamic, animated, tireless.

Many in the crowd seem to know the Stryper songs — singing the chorus of a number with the group or shouting back a slogan. Arms continue to be raised in unison with the index finger held up. A few dance, but most stay glued to the stage.

Between one song, Michael tells the crowd, "We've found you don't need drugs or booze. We've got something better — Jesus." The moment is brief and the band is quickly back into another song.

At 10:47 p.m., the lead singer announces: "We've got a gift for you." All four musicians throw out yellow and black striped New Testaments which land among the several hundred standing around the stage area.

Perhaps some 50 New Testaments in all are tossed out, and people dive for the tiny books wherever they are thrown. The effort of throwing out New Testaments is standard for all Stryper concerts.

Yet the 50 New Testaments given away seem a far cry from the 500 *Time* magazine suggested or even Robert Sweet's comment to *Hit Parader* magazine, January 1987 issue, "We spend about $1,000 a night on Bibles. . . ."

At 11 p.m., Michael Sweet sings a ballad, but the song's tempo quickens considerably before it ends in a clashing finish. He tells the crowd: "If it wasn't for you (pointing to the people), we wouldn't be here, and if it wasn't for Jesus Christ, none of this would be possible . . . and I've made a New Year's resolution to spread the Gospel of Jesus Christ all over the world."

A few applaud. Several cheer. But most of those around the stage mumble in seeming disagreement at his words. "Let's rock and roll," he shouts, and quickly the band is back into another body-pounding, ear-jamming song.

Michael's brief statement is as close as the group ever gets in presenting anything resembling the Gospel of Jesus Christ.

Throughout the concert, guitarist Oz Fox has danced up and down the yellow and black runway to the platform beside the drum set. Bassist Tim Gaines, a thin young man with a lone mane of blonde hair, has shaken his head continuously during the concert. My neck aches from just watching.

At one point, Michael Sweet dances over to the left side of the stage and plays an imaginary guitar across the genital area of his body while strutting and swinging his hips to the music's beat.

The group briefly leaves the stage after one of its crowd-rousing numbers only to be called back for an expected encore.

Robert Sweet is pouring a bottle of liquid over his head as he walks back to his drum set. In one fluid movement, he pulls off his yellow and black shirt with the numbers 777 on the back and hurls it toward the crowd.

The group's last song is also the title of an earlier album, *Soldiers Under Command.* As they finish, Michael Sweet shouts, "Jesus Christ rocks," and the group leaves the stage.

At 11:30 p.m., eight enormous bags of balloons hanging from the auditorium ceiling begin falling and popping before hitting the floor. The cross behind the Stryper stage setting blazes.

A young woman representing a TV station in San Francisco introduces herself to me. She's spent the afternoon interviewing the group and plans a profile soon for a program. When she hears this book is being written with Jimmy Swaggart, her lips seem to curl.

"These guys seem to really have a message," she says in Stryper's defense, "and they're sure not making any money at it."

"Well, somebody is at $18.50 a ticket," I answered.

A spotlight technician is removing earplugs from his ears. "I'm a professional . . . I do this for a living," he explains. "If I don't wear earplugs, I'll have a terrible headache tomorrow. It's happened before . . . that's why I wear them."

My eardrums seem to vibrate. It will be a full twenty-four hours before I feel as if I'm not talking inside a barrel.

People leave the auditorium like hundreds of ants fleeing a disrupted antbed. I never see the two street ministers again — nor did I ever see them passing out tracts in the concert. Outside, the misty rain falls. The limo waits for its passengers. Parents pick up their offspring.

A homeless man and woman who had been sitting on a park bench behind the auditorium are now gone. The strains of the song, "He Is Worthy to be Praised," come from a meeting room at the Holiday Inn where I've parked. It's a New Year's Eve meeting of the Christian Businessmen of Silicon Valley.

"Such a contrast," I think to myself as my wife and I stop to hear the worshipful, harmonious praise offered to God.

As we drive past the auditorium, a handful of teens — mostly girls — are standing in the alleyway around the bus and transport truck which apparently hauls Stryper, its equipment, and its crew. The faithful are waiting for a glimpse.

"What have I witnessed?" I pondered.

No question about it, I have just seen a sight-and-sound "show" by four talented young men. But far worse, I have also watched as hundreds of young people — maybe even a thousand or more — in desperate need of the Saviour walked out without *any* opportunity to receive Him, the Source of all life.

Instead of hearing a clear-cut, straightforward presentation of the Gospel, these young people have been treated to a shallow substitute — a musical Jesus who rocks and rolls. What a shame. It is an unbiblical, pitiful portrait of the humble Galilean, the sovereign Son of the Living God.

My heart aches over such misguided, unfit efforts in the name of the Lord.

CHAPTER TWO

THE ORIGINS OF MUSIC

O ur heart's desire should be to worship God; we have been designed by God for this purpose. If we don't worship God, we'll worship something or someone else.

— John Wimber from *Equipping The Saints*

It is very obvious even from the briefest look at the Bible that music was created by God for praise and worship. That is evident from the words of Revelation 4:11:

". . . for thou hast created all things, and for thy pleasure they are created and were created."

The Psalms, of course, was the first songbook. The great choirs of Jerusalem, under David's direction, would assemble together and sing these great songs. One section would sing a certain part and another would raise their voices in a responsive chord.

It is recorded in history that the children of Israel were the first people to sing, to clap, to play musical instruments, and to worship God in song. There are over 800 individual references to music in the Bible, either to singing or to the use of musical instruments. David is commonly referred to as *"the sweet singer of Israel."*

The Jewish people were an emotional people. Their worship was often characterized by great exclamations of joy, shouting, clapping hands, or the waving of arms, and at times, with tears. One can easily see these characteristics in the Psalms of David or by simply reading selected passages from the Old Testament.

Music was even used by the prophets when prophesying by the Holy Spirit. That's confirmed from the words of Samuel, the great judge and prophet of Israel.

> *". . . thou shalt meet a company of prophets coming down from the high place with a psaltery, and a tabret, and a pipe, and a harp, before them; and they shall prophesy"* (I Sam. 10:5).

The Bible uses frequent references to musical instruments such as the harp, the lyre, the tabret, and the tambourine. The word "psalms" in the Greek is *psalmos*, which means a set piece of music, a sacred song, to be accompanied with the harp or other instruments.

The word also means to celebrate divine worship with music and singing. This is the meaning of the Hebrew word translated as "psalms" in the following verses:

> *"Sing unto him, sing psalms unto him, talk ye of all his wondrous works"* (I Chron. 16:9).
> *"Let us come before his presence with thanksgiving, and make a joyful noise unto him with psalms"* (Psa. 95:2).

*"Sing unto him, sing psalms unto him: talk
ye of all his wondrous works"* (Psa. 105:2).

Praise and Worship

The Bible is literally filled with music. Again and
again, the Word of God records amazing incidents where
God's people burst forth with music and singing to honor
the exploits of the Lord on their behalf.

We read in Exodus 15 of Moses and the children of
Israel singing a song unto the Lord after their miraculous
crossing of the Red Sea. The song reflects the great joy of
God's people who have seen the hand of the Almighty in
sparing them from the host of Pharaoh's army:

*". . . I will sing unto the Lord, for he hath
triumphed gloriously: the horse and his rider
hath he thrown into the sea.*

*"The Lord is my strength and song, and he is
become my salvation: he is my God, and I will
prepare him an habitation; my father's God, and
I will exalt him . . ."* (Exo. 15:1, 2).

The song is actually nineteen verses in length, which
gives you some idea of the children of Israel's fervor to
praise God. Then, in verses twenty and twenty-one, the
Bible records how Miriam took timbrel in hand to lead the
women in a time of great rejoicing.

*"And Miriam, the prophetess, the sister of
Aaron, took a timbrel in her hand; and all the
women went out after her with timbrels and with
dances.*

*"And Miriam answered them, Sing ye to the
Lord, for he hath triumphed gloriously; the*

horse and his rider hath he thrown into the sea"
(Exo. 15:20, 21).

I Chronicles 15 records the extensive preparations arranged by David for the thousands of musicians to accompany the Ark of the Covenant on its return to Jerusalem. Verse 25 notes the dominate attitude over-shadowing this effort:

> *"So David, and the elders of Israel, and the captains over thousands, went to bring up the ark of the covenant of the Lord out of the house of Obed-edom with joy"* (I Chron. 15:25).

Scripture further records much of the preparations and the people's response to the activities:

> *"And David was clothed with a robe of fine linen, and all the Levites that bare the ark, and the singers, and Chenaniah the master of the song with the singers: David also had upon him an ephod of linen.*
> *"Thus all Israel brought up the ark of the covenant of the Lord with shouting, and with sound of the cornet, and with trumpets, and with cymbals, making a noise with psalteries and harps"* (I Chron. 15:27, 28).

I Chronicles 16:7-36 recounts the magnificent psalm which David composed to honor the Lord for His goodness in returning the Ark of the Covenant to His people. Verse 23 in that chapter observes:

> *"Sing unto the Lord, all the earth; shew forth from day to day his salvation."*

When Jesus Christ came into this world, His appearance was made known by a chorus of angels who serenaded some obscure shepherds watching their flock. God had chosen the medium of music to herald this signal event in human history — the coming of Emmanuel — *God with us.*

> *"And suddenly there was with the angel a multitude of the heavenly host praising God, and saying,*
> *"Glory to God in the highest, and on earth peace, good will toward men"* (Luke 2:13, 14).

In one of the most exceptional battle stories in the whole Bible, Jehoshaphat, king of Judah, took an unprecedented course of action to victory. The Scripture records:

> *"And when he had consulted with the people, he appointed singers unto the Lord, and that should praise the beauty of holiness, as they went out before the army, and to say, Praise the Lord; for his mercy endureth for ever.*
> *"And when they began to sing and to praise, the Lord set ambushments against the children of Ammon, Moab, and mount Seir, which were come against Judah; and they were smitten"* (II Chron. 20:21, 22).

In another instance in the New Testament, the mighty power of God was unleashed when Paul and Silas were arrested in Philippi, beaten, thrust into the inner part of the jail, and confined in wooden stocks. Then, a miracle happened.

> *"And at midnight Paul and Silas prayed, and sang praises unto God: and the prisoners heard them.*
>
> *"And suddenly there was a great earthquake, so that the foundations of the prison were shaken: and immediately all the doors were opened, and every one's bands were loosed"* (Acts 16:25, 26).

Musical Instruments

In looking at both the Old and New Testaments, it is also obvious that God has given scriptural approval to the use of musical instruments in worship. To sing with accompaniment is a command of the Word of God. The following Scriptures verify the use of musical instruments in worship:

• The righteous are commanded to use them in their worship of God (Psa. 33:1-5; Psa. 81:1-5; Psa. 98:4-9; Psa. 147:7; Psa. 149:1-4; Psa. 150:1-6).

• In the Old Testament, it was actually a law of God to use musical instruments (Psa. 81:1-4; II Chron. 29:25).

• When dedicated to God, musical instruments were called holy (Num. 31:6).

• God's glory (as recorded in II Chron. 5:11-14) came down when instruments were used with singing — and this still happens today.

• It was prophesied that musical instruments will be used in the reign of the Messiah (Psa. 87:7).

• Fifty-five Psalms were dedicated to the chief musician to be used in worship. And it was only when Israel misused them — to commit sin — that any rebuke came, as described in Psalm 32 and Amos 6.

• In heaven, we are told that the twenty-four elders and four angelic beings play harps (Rev. 5:8).

• The 144,000 Jews will also play harps in heaven (Rev. 14:1-5).

• All tribulation saints in heaven will play harps (Rev. 15:2).

• The New Testament commands their use in the church. In Ephesians 5:19 and Colossians 3:16, the saints are commanded to use psalms, hymns, and spiritual songs, and to make melody in their hearts to the Lord.

Without question, the Word of God from beginning to end has given its approval to the use of musical instruments in worship. To believe and practice otherwise would be contrary to Scripture.

The Ways of Worship

According to John Wimber, there are various ways described in the Old and New Testaments for worshiping God. Among them he lists the following:

"*Confession:* the acknowledgement of sin and guilt to a holy and righteous God."

"*Thanksgiving:* giving thanks to God for what He has done, especially for His works of creation and salvation."

"*Adoration:* praising God simply for who He is — Lord of the universe."

Throughout the Bible, worship can be seen in such forms as singing, playing musical instruments, dancing before the Lord, lifting hands, bowing down, and kneeling.

A.W. Tozer, in his book, *Worship: The Missing Jewel in the Evangelical Church,* adds a vital element to worship which the Jews of the Old Testament and the first century Christians understood — "feeling." Dr. Tozer wrote:

> Now I happen to belong to that segment of the church of Christ on earth that is not afraid of the word "feeling." We went through a long deep-freeze period at the turn of the century, when people talked about "naked faith."

They wanted to hang us out there like a coonskin drying on the door. And so they said, "Now, don't believe in feeling, brother; we don't believe in feeling. The only man who went by feeling was led astray; that was Isaac when he felt Jacob's arms and thought it was Esau."

But they forgot the woman who felt in her body that she was healed! Remember that? A person that merely goes through the form and doesn't feel anything is not worshiping.

Worship also means to "express in some appropriate manner" what you feel. Now, expressing in some appropriate manner doesn't mean that we always all express it in the same way all the time. And it doesn't mean that you will always express your worship in the same manner. But it does mean that it will be expressed in some manner.

And what will be expressed? "A humbling but delightful sense of admiring awe and astonished wonder." It is delightful to worship God, but it is also a humbling thing. And the man who has not been humbled in the presence of God will never be a worshiper of God at all. He may be a church member who keeps the rules and obeys the discipline, and who tithes and goes to conference, but he'll never be a worshiper unless he is deeply humbled.

There's an awesomeness about God which is missing in our day altogether; there's little sense of admiring awe in the church of Christ these days. "Awesome wonder and overpowering love" in the presence of that ancient Mystery, that unspeakable Majesty, which the philosophers call the *Mysterium Tremendum,* but which we call our Father which art in heaven. Now that's my definition of worship — that we are to feel something in our heart that we didn't have before we were converted; that we're going to express it in some way and it's going to be a humbling but a most enjoyable sense of admiring awe and astonished wonder and overpowering love in the Presence of that most ancient Mystery.

Dr. Tozer has focused upon one of the magnificent aspects of worship — that feeling deep in your soul. Surely that

was the emotion that must have gripped Jesus' followers on
His triumphal entry into Jerusalem in Luke 19:37, 38.

> *"And when he was come nigh, even now at
> the descent of the mount of Olives, the whole
> multitude of the disciples began to rejoice and
> praise God with a loud voice for all the mighty
> works that they had seen;*
> *"Saying, Blessed be the King that cometh in
> the name of the Lord: peace in heaven, and glory
> in the highest."*

Lucifer's Involvement in Music

While it is obvious that God is the source of music, it
must also be recognized from Ezekiel 28 that Lucifer,
before his fall, was heavily involved in music.

In the latter portion of Ezekiel 28:13, the Bible says:

> *". . . the workmanship of thy tabrets and of
> thy pipes was prepared in thee in the day that
> thou wast created."*

Many Bible scholars believe this pertains to the tremendous musical talents that God gave to Lucifer —
referring specifically to music and song.

In Isaiah 14:12, he is called Lucifer, *"son of the morning."*
In Ezekiel 28:14, he is described as *"the anointed cherub"*
who *"wast upon the holy mountain of God; thou hast
walked up and down in the midst of the stones of fire."*

In Job 38, the creation of the world is described in great
detail. When one considers verse seven — *". . . the morning stars sang together, and all the sons of God shouted for
joy"* — it is quite possible that Lucifer was the director of

the great choirs of heaven, who literally led the angelic host in songs of praise and worship when God made the world.

But Lucifer's music changed.

> *"Thine heart was lifted up because of thy beauty, thou hast corrupted thy wisdom by reason of thy brightness: I will cast thee to the ground, I will lay thee before kings, that they may behold thee"* (Ezek. 28:17).

Since that day, the devil has played a different tune and much of the world has danced to its sound. Like every good gift from God, Satan has often counterfeited and perverted God's gift of music to serve a demonic purpose. The "anointed cherub" created sounds that induced the worship of those angelic beings who fell from their heavenly estate with him.

Even God's own people gave heed to the satanic sound until the Lord declared:

> *"Take thou away from me the noise of thy songs; for I will not hear the melody of thy viols"* (Amos 5:23).

Music for Satan

Daniel 3 contains the classic example of music that was used as worship to Satan. The story focuses upon Nebuchadnezzar, the Babylonian king who set up a large monument to himself "in the plain of Dura." Then the command goes forth:

> *". . .To you it is commanded, O people, nations, and languages,*
> *"That at what time ye hear the sound of the*

*cornet, flute, harp, sackbut, psaltery, dulcimer,
and all kinds of musick, ye fall down and worship
the golden image that Nebuchadnezzar the king
hath set up:*

*"And whoso falleth not down and worship-
peth shall the same hour be cast into the midst of
a burning fiery furnace"* (Dan. 3:4-6).

That is music used in a demonic setting. It is offered
only as worship in a godless, carnal sense. Yet, who can
deny it is still music?

Though an entire Babylonian nation could be coerced
into bowing before this satanic music, Shadrach, Meshach,
and Abednego refused to heed this music. They knew it
paid homage to a false god. They would not bow. Their ears
were tuned to the Lord's melody.

The Greek Influence

The English word "music" comes from the Greek
word *mousike*, which means any art presided over by the
Muses. The Muses were Greek mythical characters considered to be a source of inspiration that would cause a person
to be absorbed in a thought and thereby would create a state
of being or mood.

Though we don't believe in Muses, we do know that
music deals with the emotions and that music can create a
state of being or a mood in a person. This is obvious in our
use of such terms as happy songs, sad songs, and other
such references.

I Samuel 16:16-23 recounts how music was used to
soothe the demonic oppression of King Saul. The king's
servants evidently knew something about the soothing
nature of music in certain instances, for the Scripture says:

> *"And it came to pass, when the evil spirit from God was upon Saul, that David took an harp, and played with his hand: so Saul was refreshed, and was well, and the evil spirit departed from him"* (verse 23).

The Christ Factor

Before Jesus Christ was born into this world to live among men — and later to die and rise again — most music was in the minor chords. All the great psalms originated by David for worship were basically in minor chords.

It should be noted that the majority of music from other parts of the world of that day was demonic in origin and had little or no melodic flow.

However, after the death and resurrection of the Lord Jesus Christ, music gradually changed from the minor chords to the majors, and only then was its full potential realized. It was as if Jesus' life, death, and resurrection opened up the hearts of men to a higher level of worship — thus the progression from the minor to the major chords.

The first popular music in the American colonies came from the church. The Pilgrim settlers particularly enjoyed singing psalms. The first book published in the colonies was the *Bay Psalm Book* in 1640. It contained translations of biblical psalms with directions on how to sing them.

If you look at the nations of this world which don't worship the Lord today, or which worship in a distorted or erroneous manner, you will find that their music has a strange and eerie sound disturbing to the western ear.

Not long ago while visiting Cairo, Egypt, I went out to walk and pray just before dark. During the walk I could hear the eerie wail of the Moslems as they worshiped and prayed. The music had no melody. It was simply a recurring pattern like a chant suggesting despair and darkness. Of course, there is no joy or victory in a false way of worship.

From this level of misguided worship, we can follow the further degeneration of musical form until it reaches its ultimate base level in lands where idol worship, animal sacrifice, and even human bondage exists. Without question, demonic influence provides the key for such worship.

Music, as we know it in western culture, stems from our Judeo-Christian heritage and was originally intended for the worship of God.

Yet, Satan — with tremendous abilities in musical knowledge given to him by God at his creation — has subverted all of this. He has enslaved hundreds of millions with drugs, alcohol, and illicit sex through demon-inspired music.

Music is an incredibly powerful tool — either in the realm of the Gospel or as a tool of darkness. It can usher one right into the presence of Almighty God or call forth the most vile, demonic activity imaginable on the face of planet earth.

The medium of music is just *that* powerful.

CHAPTER THREE

RELIGIOUS ROCK 'N' ROLL

 was using dope, marijuana, angel dust, cocaine, and heroin with pills and drinking and all I wanted to do was have orgies . . . rock 'n' roll doesn't glorify God . . . I was one of the pioneers of that music, one of the builders. I know what the blocks are made of because I built them.

— Little Richard

In the late 1960s and early 1970s, the "Jesus Movement" swept major areas of the country — Southern California in particular — and helped spawn a new musical style: so-called contemporary Christian music.

Most of the new converts in the movement were young people burned out by drugs, shifting sexual morality, and hedonistic life-styles. Soon hundreds were flocking to Costa Mesa's Calvary Chapel, pastored by Chuck Smith, and other similar churches where the long-haired, blue-jean-dressed youths were welcomed.

Part of Calvary Chapel's attraction was a Saturday night concert by different artists and musical groups in the congregation. In time, a new musical style was birthed — wedding, folk, country, and rock music with religious lyrics.

Even though the word "contemporary" is difficult to define within the Christian concept, it does imply conformity with today's worldly standards. Webster's Dictionary defines contemporary simply as "existing or occurring at the same time."

From its very beginnings, I sensed the musical form was an attempt to come as close as possible to secular rock and roll without actually using that name. Such a suggestion in the musical trend's infancy would have been unthinkable and certainly would have been widely opposed within the church.

In fact, the plug was pulled at a 1974 music festival in Pennsylvania on a singer dressed as a "cosmic cowboy" — waist-long hair, a thick, untrimmed beard, and earring — and his band of rockers. That singer's music would be considered tame by today's standards.

Yet as time passed, just as pop music shifted and changed, so did contemporary Christian music. By 1985, those artists embracing this sound had begun calling their music by what it really is — rock and roll.

> *"Every good gift and every perfect gift is from above, and cometh down from the Father of lights, with whom is no variableness, neither shadow of turning"* (James 1:17).

In considering rock and roll music, a person would have to ask himself, "Is secular rock music a good and perfect gift?" The answer to that is pretty obvious. Absolutely not!

Further, he would have to ask, "Is religious rock a good and perfect gift considering, especially, that it has its roots in secular rock?" That answer is obvious as well.

A further study gives us a picture of rock's birth.

The Origins of Rock

When rock music started back in the early 1950s, it was bad, but it was a far cry from what it has become today — vulgar, obscene, and so utterly degraded there is nothing good that can be said about it. Frank Zappa symbolized the rock message in *Life* magazine, saying, "Rock music is sex."

In detailing the origins of rock music, Ira Peck, in the book, *The New Sound Yes,* wrote:

> There in the late 1930s in the fields and shanties of the delta country, evolved an earthy, hard-driving style of music called "rhythm and blues" — played by blacks for blacks. Cured in misery, it was a lonesome, soul-sad music full of cries and wails punctuated by a heavy, regular beat.

Songs like "Good Rockin' Tonight" and "Rock Around the Clock" no doubt effected the terminology of the music, but a Cleveland disc jockey, Alan Freed, was the man who actually coined the term.

Freed, who was one of the first whites to play rhythm and blues over the radio, didn't know what to call this wild music that caused girls — sitting in the front row of concerts — to become frantic . . . screaming, crying, and trying to rip the clothes off some of the performers.

The disc jockey, who was later indicted in the payola scandals, finally borrowed the term "rock and roll" which was a ghetto expression sometimes used to mean sexual intercourse. The term, of course, characterized the wickedness inherent in this new music craze.

I doubt I'll ever forget that period because my cousin Jerry Lee Lewis was one of the prime movers in the birth of rock and roll as a musical form. Jerry Lee, Elvis Presley, Chuck Berry, and Little Richard were the first superstars of the movement.

It was Presley who gave the music national exposure when he stepped before one of the largest TV audiences of that day on the Ed Sullivan Show and belted out one of his songs such as "Don't Be Cruel" or "Hound Dog."

With his hair flapping in his face, his hips gyrating, and his voice charged with emotion, he was considered so sensual at one time that one or two of Sullivan's programs televised his performance from a camera angle at the waist up.

The New Sound Yes said about Presley:

> He outraged adult sensibilities. But the more parents, moralists, clergymen, and critics railed against him, the more teenagers flipped for him. Elvis was, for them, the supreme symbol of juvenile rebellion.

Sam Phillips, owner of Sun Records in Memphis, who first recorded Elvis, was quoted as saying: "I've found a white man who sings like a black." Musical history had been made.

Presley not only created a stir on television when he appeared, but riots broke out in a number of towns where he performed. Rock concerts were banned in some cities. Finally, a Senate subcommittee began investigating the link between rock music and juvenile delinquency.

A Prophecy

About the same time rock and roll music was launched, a peculiar event occurred during a Pentecostal church service in Canada. People were coming to the altar for prayer when a young woman suddenly fell to the floor and began writhing like a snake and making hissing sounds.

The church's pastor immediately moved to where the girl lay and attempted to rebuke the demonic oppression. Yet there was no visible effect to his efforts.

He stepped back momentarily and prayed, "Lord, what's wrong? I don't understand why the oppression isn't lifted from this girl."

The Lord spoke to the pastor: "Rebuke the spirit for what it is . . . call it a *counterfeit* of the Holy Ghost."

When the pastor took that bold step, a profane spirit suddenly spoke from the girl before she was set free. "I am a prince and I have come down . . . I have come down to possess a race . . . the youth of the world."

Without question, what has happened in the last thirty years has been nothing more than the youth of this world being possessed by demons — through rock music.

Death in the Music

Elvis — the so-called "king of rock" — became a victim of the culture when he died of a drug overdose in August 1977. His personal physician admitted that Presley gobbled up vast amounts of drugs ". . . from the time he woke up in the morning until the time he went to sleep at night."

Jerry Lee, as well as Chuck Berry, continues to perform even though my cousin has been near death a number of times because of his life-style. Little Richard has made several public professions of faith in Christ over the years — even holding revival meetings for a time. But at last report, he was singing what he called "message" music and recently appeared in a cameo role in the movie, "Down and Out in Beverly Hills."

Still, the music they helped create has persisted over the years and today destroys more lives than ever.

It all started out with what might today be referred to as "plain rock" or basic rock and roll. This was the carefree, "let's party" music of the 1950s.

This soon deteriorated into "hard rock" — the music of the mid to late 1960s characterized by groups from England such as the Beatles, the Rolling Stones, the Animals, and others.

Eight years after Elvis had appeared on the Ed Sullivan Show — February 1964 — the Beatles appeared before an estimated 60 million people, one of the largest TV audiences in history. The group, with its heavy, amplified music, long hair, undersized suits, high-heeled boots, and tight harmonies, was an instant hit.

The Rolling Stones' tenth album, *Beggar's Banquet*, released in December 1968 after wrangling with their record company over the public toilet cover art, charted new ground for rock and roll. The album's opening song was entitled "Sympathy for the Devil" and would influence rock groups, album concepts, and musical influence for years to come.

In the late 1960s, during the time of the Vietnam war, the rock message centered around anti-establishment themes of protest, violence, drugs, and sex. Rock artists such as Bob Dylan, Creedence Clearwater Revival, and Crosby, Stills, and Nash became immensely popular.

In observing the changes in our society then, *Time* magazine stated in its February 22, 1971, edition:

> The counterculture sprang more than anything else from rock-n-roll music. The shattering, obliterating volume . . . amounted to a new form of violence . . . coupled with the anarchic, brute-sexual rhythm and lyrics of rock-n-roll music. The counterculture is the world's first

socio-political movement to grow out of the force of electronically amplified music.

An "acid rock" phase of the music came along in the late 1960s and early 1970s influenced by the continual portrayal of drugs in rock lyrics. Groups such as the Jefferson Airplane and the Grateful Dead popularized this sound.

Three of rock's best-known performers — Jimi Hendrix, Janis Joplin, and Jim Morrison — all died within a matter of months of each other. Hendrix, who played the guitar in what he called "a big flash of weaving and bobbing, and groping and maiming, and attack," died of a drug overdose in September 1970.

A short two weeks later, Joplin, who had climbed to fame as a young blues singer with Big Brother and the Holding Company, was found with her head split open from a fall, after overdosing on heroin. At her death, her body was riddled with syphilis.

In the book, *Freakshow,* writer Albert Goldman described Morrison:

> Abundantly gifted as a singer and songwriter, Morrison is, above all, a powerfully seductive public personality, at his most entrancing, onstage . . . Morrison — in any of his aspects — is energized by a ferocious eroticism. Totally uninhibited he appears to be always in a state of smoldering and eruptive sexual excitement.

After a brief, but highly successful, career as lead singer of the Doors, Morrison quit the group and moved to Paris. His body, already wrecked by alcohol, caused his heart to quit. In July 1971 he died in his bath. He was 28.

The early to late 1970s became the era of the super groups such as Led Zeppelin, Pink Floyd, Deep Purple, and the Who. These bands drew thousands of young people to their concerts in the world's largest stadiums and coliseums.

In the late 1970s came the ear-shattering heavy metal groups such as Iron Maiden, Black Sabbath, KISS, AC/DC, and Van Halen. Many of these bands are still around today, along with groups such as Motley Crue, Ozzy Osborne, and Bon Jovi. The direction behind such heavy metal bands' music is sex, drugs, and satanism.

Rock's trend today is towards punk or the new wave sound. It is characterized by groups like Plasmatics, New York Dolls, and Talking Heads, who project rebellion against parental authority, anarchy, and bodily perversion — much of it more extreme than simple pornography.

Nihilism is the binding force behind punk rockers. It's the belief that there is no meaning or purpose in existence. These people who embrace such music generally reject all customary beliefs in morality, religion, and social standards. Punk rockers stand for nothing more than total rebellion against society.

Punk rock has a constant reference to violence, and violence is nothing more than worship to Satan.

Alfred Aronowitz, former music critic for the *New York Post*, has written:

> If the establishment knew what today's popular music is really saying, not only what the words are saying but what the music itself is saying, then they wouldn't just turn thumbs down on it. They'd ban it, they'd smash all the records, and they'd arrest anyone who tried to play it.

Rock's Relation to Religion

As far as the music was concerned, 1950s-style rock music was little different from some of the music that had been played in various church services over the years. That may sound strange to some people but it is, nonetheless, true.

In fact, virtually all of the early stars of rock music were all products of either the church itself or had gospel music backgrounds. Among them were Elvis Presley, Jerry Lee Lewis, Little Richard, Ray Charles, Sam Cooke, Roy Hamilton, Pat Boone, and Marvin Gaye. The list could cover several pages if I listed all the individuals.

This 1950s-style rock was basically done in four-four time with double measure used on some songs. If a person went back to the old Billy Sunday crusades 75 or 80 years ago with the great choirs led by Homer Rodeheaver, he would have heard basically the same rhythm patterns.

It wouldn't have had the same impact, of course, simply because they didn't have the electric instrumentation we do now, but the rhythm patterns were the same.

People by the thousands would clap their hands and sing "Brighten the Corner Where You Are" or "When We All Get to Heaven" and enjoy themselves immensely in the Lord.

However, it was the same rhythm pattern that Elvis Presley and my cousin Jerry Lee were singing. So the music wasn't new. In fact, I believe it drew much of its influence from the church. In many full-gospel churches, the same type of musical worship was carried on and has been at least part of the success of the great Pentecostal form of worship.

Rhythm within itself is not wrong. It's only when it's used incorrectly that the problem arises.

Man is a tripartite being — spirit, soul, and body. In this triune being there is another complex creation of God. It is harmonic, melodic, and rhythmic.

The harmonic area of man deals with music but also relates to speech and thought patterns. The harmonic part of man functions within the spirit realm.

The melodic, or melody, relates to the soul and affects the lyrical and cadence of speech within man.

The rhythmic or rhythm relates to the flesh of man — his physical body.

All of this represents God's creation and stands together as a part of man's spiritual, physical, and psychological makeup. As such, within themselves, they are not evil.

However, these portions of man's being can be perverted to the point where the natural senses become degraded and cease to worship God and, instead, worship or cater to the devil or to the wicked impulses of the flesh.

For instance, when the children of Israel crossed the Red Sea, they played tambourines and had a camp meeting on the shores of that great waterway. They danced before the Lord in great joy.

It's virtually impossible to play a tambourine without doing so in a rhythmic fashion. Consequently, these Israelites who had just witnessed a mighty miracle from God were playing in rhythm. Of course, it was sanctioned by the Holy Spirit.

There are seven basic words that described ancient Jewish worship as found in the Old Testament and which have been carried over into the New Testament. One of these words is *zamar*, which means "to touch the strings."

This word is used in connection with instrumental worship. It has to do with percussion, wind, or rhythm instruments. Examples are found in Psalm 57:9 and Psalm 150.

The Greek word for "psalms" in James 5:13 is *psallo*, which means to "twitch or twang, or to play on a stringed instrument."

So rhythm within itself is not wrong. Even though this element of rhythm may be in rock, pop, folk, or even gospel music, it constitutes nothing wrong as such. Unless the music overpowers the message, then the rhythm becomes all-important. Then the music takes on an entirely different complexion.

The Rhythm of Rock

In noting man's rhythmic physical nature, Dr. John Diamond observed that man is rhythmic in respiration, heartbeat, pulse, speech, and gait. When the rhythm of music corresponds to the natural body rhythms, he suggested, it produces ecstasy, alertness, and peace, energizes the mind and body, and facilitates balance and self-control.

Dr. David Nobel, a music authority reporting on the value of music rhythms corresponding to body rhythms, has written:

> None of these qualities accrue to the rock sound. Instead, rock contains harmonic dissonance and melodic discord while it accents rhythm with a big beat. In fact, the anapestic beat used by many rock musicians actually is the exact opposite of our heart and arterial rhythms."

Dr. Diamond reported that the stopped anapestic rhythm "heightens stress and anger, reduces output, increases hyperactivity, and weakens muscle strength."

Music composer and conductor Dimitri Tiomkin said of the rock sound: ". . . Youngsters who listen constantly to this sort of sound are thrust into turmoil. They are no longer relaxed, normal kids."

What these professionals are saying is that today's rock sound fights against the rhythmic nature of man's creation.

Rock — the Destroyer

Rock and roll, both the music and the life-style, has literally trapped and destroyed the lives of millions of people. The death count of the rock musicians themselves, who have succumbed over the years to their own life-styles, would cover page after page if I began listing the names and describing their destructive fates.

Just a brief look at the individuals who died from drug overdoses or from alcohol-related deaths resulting in suffocation from vomit would include the following:

Tommy Bolin (1950-1975), from Deep Purple and James
                    Gang
Tim Buckley (1947-1975)
Nick Drake (1948-1974)
Tim Hardin (1940-1980)
Jimi Hendrix (1942-1970)
Gregory Herbert (1950-1978), from Blood, Sweat, and
                    Tears
Janis Joplin (1943-1970)
Frankie Lymon (1942-1968)
Robbie McIntosh (1944-1974), from Average White Band
Keith Moon (1946-1978), from the Who
Gram Parsons (1946-1973)
Elvis Presley (1935-1977)
Sid Vicious (1958-1979), from the Sex Pistols
Bon Scott (1947-1980), from AC/DC
Danny Whitten (1945-1972), from Crazy Horse
Alan Wilson (1943-1970), from Canned Heat
John Bonham (1948-1980), from Led Zeppelin.

The list of rock and rollers who committed suicide would include the following persons:

Johnny Ace (1929-1954)
Ian Curtis (1959-1980), from Joy Division
Peter Ham (1947-1975), from Bad Finger
Donny Hathaway (1945-1979)

Phil Ochs (1940-1976)
Rory Storme (1940-1974)
Paul Williams (1939-1973), from the Temptations.

Of course, names missing from this listing would include the eleven young people who were trampled to death at a 1979 Who concert in Cincinnati. They were trapped inside a crowd surging to get inside the coliseum and were crushed under the feet of the uncontrolled mob.

Also not included would be the five people, knifed or beaten to death by the Hell's Angels motorcycle gang, hired as security guards for a free Rolling Stones concert at Altamont Motor Speedway outside San Francisco in 1969.

The list does not include the 1,600 teenagers who attempt suicide every day — some of which succeed. Nor does it contain the millions of young people whose lives have been wrecked — and some destroyed — because of drugs, illicit sex, or satanism championed by rock and roll music.

The music and its accompanying life-style is *the* predominate influence in the life of a typical teenager. Its influence overshadows family, school, and church. Rock stars are the heroes to this generation.

Yet rock music is one of the most destructive forces in this nation. As Dr. David Nobel correctly stated, it is nothing more than "pornography set to music."

It seems absolutely inconceivable to me that any group which considers itself Christian would accept the rock and roll designation — especially when one considers the horror that has been imposed on generation after generation by this form of music.

Yet there are many performers who boldly proclaim their Christianity while still openly professing they are also rock and rollers. Mylon LeFevre is one such person.

"I'm a Rock and Roller"

Contemporary Christian Magazine's profile on Mylon LeFevre, in its March 1986 edition, quotes Mylon as saying:

> Our music is rock and roll. We don't even tell anybody it's contemporary Christian music . . . We are a rock 'n' roll band. We sound like one, we look like one, and at the end of the night we smell like one. . . .

As a youngster Mylon performed with his parents' southern gospel group and he wrote popular gospel songs. Fired from the group in a dispute over the length of his sideburns, Mylon took the opportunity to record some rock songs he had written but the family wouldn't record.

What followed were years of heroin addiction and recording and performing with some of the world's most famous rock musicians. He made a full surrender of his life to Christ in April 1980 and returned to Christian music in 1982. But evidently a change has come about.

In describing what he does now, Mylon stated:

> It's a rock 'n' roll show that is a ministry. You can't separate the two. Rock 'n' roll is what I do. I put on a good show. I entertain those people. I have a good time with them. . . .

Rock and roll is a ministry? I would have to ask the question, "What type of ministry?" For someone to suggest that rock and roll is the same as biblical ministry has to be the most far-out statement that could ever be uttered.

Earlier we have described the origins of rock and roll. It should be obvious as to what rock and roll is and what it has done in millions of lives. By simply adding the word

"Christian" does not change anything, nor does attempting to justify it as "ministry." That is little more than blasphemy or total ignorance.

To prove my point, look at these sentences: *"I put on a good show. I entertain those people. I have a good time with them. . . ."*

Can you imagine the Apostle Paul "putting on a good show"?

What type of "entertainment" do you think Simon Peter engaged in?

Is there anything in the Bible, and more specifically, is there anything in the New Testament that has to do with "putting on a good show," "entertaining people," and "having a good time with them"?

> *"And it was about the sixth hour, and there was a darkness over all the earth until the ninth hour.*
>
> *"And the sun was darkened, and the vail of the temple was rent in the midst.*
>
> *"And when Jesus had cried with a loud voice, he said, Father, into thy hands I commend my spirit: and having said thus, he gave up the ghost"* (Luke 23:44-46).
>
> *". . . in labours more abundant, in stripes above measure, in prisons more frequent, in deaths oft.*
>
> *"Of the Jews five times received I forty stripes save one.*
>
> *"Thrice was I beaten with rods, once was I stoned, thrice I suffered shipwreck, a night and a day I have been in the deep"* (II Cor. 11:23-25).

Upon a simple investigation, I believe it would be very difficult to coincide a "good show" or "entertainment" or a "good time" with the passages I have quoted.

Destiny magazine interviewed Mylon for an article on contemporary Christian music in its May/June 1986 issue. In answer to a question, "Why do you keep playing this loud music to teenagers? You're forty-one years old," Mylon said in part:

> . . . I was a rock 'n' roller for twenty-five years, and what God showed me is I am now a "born-again, Spirit-filled, rock 'n' roller who has been called to preach and teach and make disciples."

Communicating Truth

I have no problem with Mylon's Christian convictions or his heart motives. All of those can be correct — as with any individual — and yet their methods can be totally wrong, even foreign to the Gospel.

It is my conviction that rock music cannot be used to communicate spiritual truth. I cannot possibly see how rock music, with its origins in demonic activities, can apply to the Gospel of the Lord Jesus Christ.

Convictions must be based on the Word of God and not personal tastes, likes, and dislikes. Most of religious rock or so-called contemporary Christian music draws its inspiration from secular rock and roll. The result is worldliness in the music — and even worse, worldliness *through* music invading the church. Further, it authenticates the rock sound by having people who are supposed to be Christians playing the music.

Thus, when I apply the standards of the Bible to this form of worldliness, I recognize the wrongness of such music. The Scripture states in the following places:

> *"Wherefore come out from among them, and*
> *be ye separate, saith the Lord, and touch not the*

unclean thing . . ." (II Cor. 6:17).
    "Abstain from all appearance of evil"
(I Thess. 5:22).
    "And be not conformed to this world . . ."
(Rom. 12:2).

When I consider these Scriptures in the light of where rock and roll came from and the evil influence it has had in destroying millions of lives, there is no question in my mind: religious rock has no place in the church of the Lord Jesus Christ.

MUSIC FOR EVANGELISM

I am a Christian, so nothing I ever do is secular. Even when I sing a pop song that doesn't mention Jesus, it's still a Christian song because I'm representing it. If it's played on a secular radio station, then they are playing a Christian song if they know it or not. My art form to communicate to people is rock and roll.

— British singer Cliff Richard

The heart of the matter as it relates to religious rock is that people have brought a musical form, birthed in the seething cauldron of rebellion, into the church and attempted to identify it as a tool of evangelism.

Music is *not* for evangelism.

There is no biblical case for music to be used for evangelism as some proponents of religious rock would suggest. In fact, there is not one scriptural reference in the Bible tying music and evangelism together.

Music in the Bible in every instance is either used in praise and worship to God or to Satan. There appears to be no biblical ground for the use of music as a viable soul-winning technique.

Gospel music has always been meant to prepare people's hearts for the preaching of God's Word. Throughout history, individuals with gospel music ministries have always been connected to preaching ministries.

The Bible states clearly in I Corinthians 1:21:

> ". . . it pleased God by the foolishness of preaching to save them that believe."

Evangelism, or soul winning, is always tied into the preaching of the Word. Although mentioned over 800 times in Scripture, music is never used as entertainment or an end within itself. The music medium can speak to us, soothe and challenge us, but it takes the preaching of the Gospel to transform a life.

Yet the religious rockers are steadfastly maintaining that the reason for their approach — manner of dress, sound systems, strobe lights — is solely for the purpose of soul-winning.

Mylon LeFevre is quoted as saying:

> A light show, flashy dress, and large sound systems are not used to urge Christians to come to the concerts. Those things are used to attract the unsaved to come so we can give them Jesus, the Word of God. Before you can teach people the Gospel, you have to get them to come to the auditorium where you are holding a concert.
>
> For that reason, the sound of the band members and the looks are very important. That's the only reason Broken Heart looks and sounds the way it does. If I could be a regular preacher and still reach kids, I would.

Ironically, most of these singers and musicians now playing religious rock were *not* won to Jesus Christ by the same tactics they now claim must be employed to reach young people. They weren't saved on a rock and roll gospel.

Yet virtually all these artists — some of which sport mohawk haircuts and wear chains and leather — insist that young people can be reached *only* through the medium of their culture, rock music.

The basic truth is that these individuals like the trendy clothing of the youth culture and they enjoy rock music. That's why they've adopted such tactics. *It has very little to do with soul-winning since most of their efforts are directed at church kids who are already born again.*

Thousands for Christ

Mylon LeFevre indicated in a published interview that some 30,000 young people had signed a card during a year's time indicating they had given their lives to Christ following a religious rock concert by his group, Broken Heart.

My question is this: Where are these young people today? What has happened since they supposedly signed a card? Have they been discipled? Did someone help them find a Bible-believing local church? Did anybody do any follow-up on all of these so-called conversions?

Any valid evangelism program to reach people for the Lord Jesus will have a sensible follow-up program to enable the new converts to grow and mature in the faith. Without it, an individual has been done a great disservice. He has not been blessed.

A Baton Rouge Experience

I would ask these religious rockers who feel their music is enabling them to win the lost — how do you reach the unsaved when a Christian promoter books the groups, Christian radio stations advertise the concerts, and Christian bookstores sell the tickets to other Christians?

How?

In essence, religious rock artists are banking on young people, some of whom have never shared their faith with anybody, to give them a perfect musical setting to bring their unsaved friends. It just doesn't happen.

Glen Berteau, youth pastor at Family Worship Center in Baton Rouge, took a poll this past summer of the young people attending the weekly Crossfire meeting. He asked how many had been saved through a church service or attendance at a Christian camp?

About 70 percent of the kids raised their hands.

He then asked how many had been saved through one-on-one witnessing from another Christian. Almost all of the remaining young people in the auditorium raised their hands.

He asked finally how many had been saved at a religious rock concert. Only one person out of approximately 800 young people (in attendance that night) raised his hand.

After the service, the young man told Glen he had given his life to Christ five years earlier at a concert. The teenager's cousin had witnessed to him prior to the concert; thus his heart had already been prepared.

Yet the trend persists. Religious rockers claim the only reason for their approach — the loud music, the rock outfits styled after the world, the theatrics on stage — is to win converts for Jesus.

From all the information I've received, the religious rockers aren't reaching new converts for Christ. They're making disciples to their rock music style out of church kids because that's 95 percent of their audience.

Altar Calls

It is obvious that if the religious rockers are presenting the Gospel of the Lord Jesus, then there must be an opportunity for the hearers to respond. That's basic with any evangelistic service.

Yet Amy Grant, who has sold more than four million records and been arguably called *"the most popular Christian singer on the face of the earth,"* does not give altar calls in her concerts.

In discussing her album, *Unguarded*, she gives a hint at her emphasis:

> I wanted to make a record that would basically fit between Madonna and Huey Lewis.

Perhaps this emphasis is why the *Chicago Sun Times*, in its March 23, 1986, edition, dubbed her "the Madonna of Christian Rock." One publication noted:

> The lyrics on much of this new album deliver their message in a much subtle way. The words "Jesus," "Lord," and "God" come up less often, and Grant has even included a straightforward love song.

She is quoted in another article from *U.S. News & World Report* as saying:

> If you are really searching for something, my music will speak to you.

How does she think her music will speak to you? She's using the tactics *and* the music of the world. If a person is really searching for Jesus Christ, there's virtually no way he could find Him in anything this young lady does.

Jesus declared the following about His presentation of the *"Good News"*:

> *". . . I spake openly to the world; I ever taught in the synagogue, and in the temple, whither the Jews always resort; and in secret have I said nothing"* (John 18:20).

Why wouldn't a Christian want to proclaim Jesus openly? I can't understand the reason for not telling the world about Him. That's the approach He took in preaching His message.

Of course, I know some people will say Jimmy Swaggart isn't in the modern era. He's somewhere back in the 1950s. If that's your thinking, then read the following letter written to *Contemporary Christian Magazine* from a 17-year-old girl in Charleston, S.C.

> I'm writing regarding Bob Darden's review of Amy Grant's latest album, *Unguarded* (June). As a 17-year-old Christian surrounded by "the world," I feel what I have to say is relevant.
>
> What message is Amy taking to this "dying world"? I've heard her album and have also heard "Love Will Find a Way" on both Christian and secular radio stations. I don't see any message except, as your review put it, "a positive, ethical life-style . . . without preaching." A positive, ethical life-style is nothing more than humanism. Yes, *her* message has gotten through to this lost and dying world. Perhaps that is the problem — it's Amy's message and not God's.

Amen, young lady, you've put your finger exactly on the root of the problem.

"Between Heaven 'n' Hell"

Rez Band, a Chicago-based religious rock band, affiliated with a Christian community in the inner city, is a case in point of a musical group who shapes its appearance and sound based on punk or new wave rock.

A recent profile in the book, *The Heart of Rock and Roll,* noted the following about the group:

> Guitarist Glenn Kaiser and drummer John Herrin, both pastors in a local Christian community, are leading a rhythmic assault on the ears and bodies of the people in the audience.
>
> Glenn slashes at his guitar like he's fighting off a six-stringed attacker, while John throws his sticks at his drums. Stu Heiss on guitar and John Denton on bass add their instruments to the musical mix. Then Wendi Kaiser belts out her harsh vocals to the first verse of a song that paints a bleak picture of the emptiness of modern life:
>> Hiding out in my bedroom,
>> I wish that I could die:
>> No one seems to love me,
>> But I'm not going to cry.

In describing the group, Glenn Kaiser is quoted as saying:

> We look at ourselves as a band that just happens to be Christian. We are Christians first, and we make no bones about the fact that we follow Jesus and that we are speaking from a biblical perspective. But at the same time we are no longer afraid to be known as rock and roll musicians.

For this group to talk about following Jesus in the same breath with boasting about being a rock and roll musician is an oxymoron. It's like trying to combine oil and water, light and darkness, sin and salvation. It *cannot* be done.

What they are advocating is something in biblical terminology that does not exist.

The Word of God looks at these issues with the following instructions:

> *"Wherefore come out from among them, and be ye separate, saith the Lord, and touch not the unclean thing; and I will receive you"* (II Cor. 6:17).

> *". . . choose you this day whom ye will serve . . . but as for me and my house, we will serve the Lord"* (Josh. 24:15).

A sympathetic article (April 1986) in *Contemporary Christian Magazine* about this religious rock group states:

> While undeniably popular among Christian rock fans, Rez has, since its inception in 1972, been periodically targeted by the church's right-wing factions as immoral, as evil influences, as messengers of Satan, and other such tripe. With their latest career move, the band now runs the risk of alienating even their staunchest allies in the world of Christian rock — but it's a risk worth taking.

Just what kind of questions would the average Christian raise about a religious rock band interested in a good "career move"? It simply sounds like somebody attempting to carve a bigger piece of the pie for themselves.

The article explains just what kind of "career move" this religious rock band is taking:

> A new album, *Between Heaven 'N' Hell* [their eighth], recently hit the streets, and with it, Rez begins its campaign aimed at winning over the secular mainstream rock audience. Last fall, their label, Sparrow Records,

signed a distribution agreement with Capitol Records — a much-vaunted improvement over Sparrow's previous alliance with MCA.

Capitol will not only manufacture Sparrow discs, but it will lend its radio promotion staff to help get them played on secular radio stations. So far, *Between Heaven 'N' Hell* has seen airplay on a number of AOR (album-oriented rock) stations in Texas, including Dallas' formidable KZEW-FM.

Rez has made a number of other moves designed to facilitate their transition to the secular market. They've pacted with a New York-based management/marketing firm on a four-month trial basis. They have signed with the venerable Diversified Management Agency (DMA) out of Detroit who will be handling concert bookings. (Other heavy DMA clients include the Scorpions, Quiet Riot, and Autograph.) And they've been concentrating more on videos, resulting in MTV's picking up *Love Comes Down*, the band's latest video effort as well as their latest single release.

No doubt this religious rock group will have to adopt some changes in this big switch. I wonder if any of the changes will be significant? The article continues:

> The members of Rez band realize their secular move is double jeopardy: they might be rejected by the non-Christian rock establishment for their religious roots and their old fans might take exception to their taking on the world.
> . . . In order to do that, Rez is all too aware, they're going to have to "play by certain rules," as Herrin puts it. *They've already stopped the practice of altar calls in concert, and they're toning down overt references to the Lord. In general, they want to present themselves, first and foremost, as a rock band.* (Italics mine.)

Do you recognize a trend developing with the religious rockers? Some are quitting the practice of altar calls. Most are dropping clear-cut references to the Lord. The emphasis is on raw rock and roll.

Jesus declared about Himself:

"And I, if I be lifted up from the earth, will draw all men unto me" (John 12:32).

The Word of God does not say adopt the tactics, methods, and styles of a rock band.

Can Jesus be really lifted up at a rock concert? Can anyone be genuinely converted while these rock musicians scream their message and play their blaring instruments? The audience won't even know the purpose for any of this so-called "sanctified entertainment."

Contemporary Christian Magazine's article noted that:

> . . . Rez had gotten the distinct impression that they were preaching primarily to the converted.

If that's the case, why has this group been attempting to convince Christians for the last twelve years they were playing their brand of music and dressing as they did to reach lost souls? Did it honestly take them that long to reach such a conclusion?

In truth, an altar call does not fit the setting for what most of these groups create. It would be like casting pearls before swine (Matthew 7:6). An altar call should be given when the Spirit of God is present, moving with conviction to touch the hearts and lives of people.

The Spirit of God is not in such concerts, so why give an altar call?

". . . That's Not My Calling"

Michael W. Smith, a talented keyboard musician who has played on a number of Amy Grant's records and also written several popular praise songs, was aided on his new album by producer John Potoker, who produced records for Paul McCartney, Phil Collins, the Thompson Twins, and Mick Jagger.

On Smith's newest album, *The Big Picture*, he has sprinkled fewer overt religious references and has omitted from the LP any praise songs. He figures the best way to take this message to young people is "wrap it up in a package they would want to open."

Regarding his concerts, (*Contemporary Christian Magazine*/June 1986), Smith is quoted as saying:

> The people coming into the concerts are ready to rock. They come out and want to have a good time. Some people need to get out there and preach to them. Ask them for a decision at the end, but that's not my calling. The kids I see are just ready to kick it out and have fun.

I'm frankly amazed that anyone feels his calling in life is "to rock." If the music is supposed to be about Christ, why wouldn't there be an opportunity to receive Him? Would somebody's conversion mess up the program?

Somehow the music has become more important than either the Messiah or the message. To be frank with you, Jesus Christ was never the purpose. He was only the pawn in this money game.

Reaching the Kids

All of these religious rockers will tell you their number one goal is to reach the kids with their music and/or their message. Perhaps we need to re-define the word "reach."

My concept of "reach" is to extend an opportunity for non-believers to know the Lord Jesus Christ. Webster's Dictionary says reach means "to stretch out" or "to extend."

I am totally mystified how anyone can be *reached* with the Gospel when the music dominates the message . . . when the name of Jesus is no longer mentioned . . . when no altar call is given . . . and when the style of the musicians and singers becomes the focal point of the entire concert.

Such presentations, programs, and albums have nothing to do with the Gospel. No tangible, worthwhile result can be achieved because the Lord Jesus Christ has not been lifted up. That scriptural method — by lifting up the Son of God — is the only proven way to ever get any results.

Religious rocker Steve Taylor went so far as to criticize another contemporary singer, Carman, for establishing some criteria for a concert. Taylor is quoted in the February 1986 issue of *Contemporary Christian Magazine* as saying:

> . . . I heard the other day that Carman had come up with four criteria for Christian concerts that he shares. One was that you had to talk about a literal devil, one was that you had to give an altar call, and I can't remember the other two. Now Carman's an intelligent guy. Where does he get off laying down these rules?

I'd suggest a good place — the Bible. It's a place many of the religious rockers have drifted far from.

CHAPTER
FIVE

MIXING THE
SACRED AND SEXY

ou don't need the devil to teach you music. People said when I came to the Lord, "Now you can use all this talent and what you've learned over the years for the Lord." Listen, it took me six years to unlearn what I learned from the world!
— Carman in concert, January 25, 1987, Decatur, GA

One of the greatest elements lacking with the so-called contemporary Christian music is an incredible void of understanding of the holiness of God and the responsibility of singers and musicians to communicate that.

The words of Ezekiel 44:23 cry out for recognition:

"And they shall teach my people the dif- ference between the holy and profane, and cause them to discern between the unclean and the clean."

Instead of God being exalted or some facet of Christ's glorious character and redemption being praised, we are often treated to a sensual, secular glorification of the flesh which looks, sounds, and appears as nothing more than an instrument of Hollywood.

Since 1975, a Christian Artists Music Seminar has been held during the summer at Estes Park, Colorado. *Newsweek* magazine (August 19, 1985) took note of the 1985 gathering.

> . . . At the Estes Park concert, Britain's Sheila Walsh — who has her own BBC television show — artfully mixed the sacred and sexy. Emerging from clouds of machine-made smoke on a darkened stage — at these concerts, there are no drafts of marijuana fumes — Walsh held her arms out to form a shadowy crucifix. But when the beat quickened, bright lights suddenly revealed a strutting Walsh in shiny white spandex pants, an oversize white shirt, white lace gloves, and glittered hair. Her message was arresting, too: songs of troubled marriages and fear of nuclear war.

Can you tell me why so-called Christian entertainers are even mixing what a secular magazine like *Newsweek* calls the "sacred and sexy"? What does that kind of sensuality have to do with the Gospel of Jesus Christ?

What about the Christian virtues of righteousness, purity, and holiness? Are those biblical traits out of style in the 1980s?

I once heard A.N. Trotter say, *"The reason people do such things is that they do not understand the holiness of God."*

Yet this brand of sensuality runs the length and breadth of religious rock. It is a disgrace in the eyes of God.

Amy Grant and *Rolling Stone*

Amy Grant's controversial June 1985 interview in *Rolling Stone* magazine produced a flood of criticism from fans, ministers, and Christian bookstore owners to her management company and her record company.

Rolling Stone reporter Michael Goldberg wrote:

> Grant's also pragmatic about her career. Regarding her album covers and publicity photos, which portray her as a sexy, attractive young woman. The Christian pop star says, *"I'm trying to look sexy to sell a record.* But what is sexy? To me it's never been taking my shirt off or sticking my tongue out. *I feel that a Christian young woman in the eighties is very sexual."* (Italics mine.)

Word Records spokesman Scott Pelking said the record company had received numerous complaints about Ms. Grant's "harsh" language quoted in the interview, especially her comments about sex.

The *Rolling Stone* article also raised eyebrows over a reference to Amy Grant sunbathing in the nude, as well as comments, some sexually explicit, about a Prince concert she attended.

The *Rolling Stone* story gave the following quote:

> . . . "When he [Prince] started humping the stage, I got a little embarrassed," says the twenty-four-year-old Grant, sitting in the bright sunlight near the swimming pool at her Universal City hotel. "I quit looking."
>
> "When he thrust his crotch up into the florescent shower," she continues in her Southern drawl, "I thought if someone wants to do this at home, fine. If I want to do this at home, fine. I don't want to watch Prince doing it. I didn't get off watching him create the illusion of masturbating."

The Word Records spokesman said the complaints about her language were being answered with, "That's the way she is. She's very frank."

Her manager, brother-in-law Dan Harrell, was quoted as saying, "Amy is as committed as ever to minister to kids who don't know Jesus," adding, "If God's judgment is going to fall on us for that, let it fall."

The article, Harrell claimed, is "inflammatory," but the most distressing part for Amy is to see a lack of love and understanding from Christians.

Isn't it ironic, if you ever question someone's published remarks or somehow challenge their point of view, you're always accused of "lacking love."

On the contrary, I think it *is* an act of love to tell people there will be no mixing the sacred and sexy in heaven. *It is wrong!* It has no basis in Christianity. God is not its author.

The Apostle Paul declared in Galatians 4:16:

> *"Am I therefore become your enemy, because I tell you the truth?"*

Donnie's Conversation

Several days after the *Rolling Stone* article was printed, Amy Grant's 1985 tour was underway and came to Baton Rouge. My son, Donnie, who had been acquainted previously with Amy's husband, Gary Chapman, went to the concert with Glen Berteau, youth pastor of Family Worship Center.

Knowing how the secular news media can twist and distort stories on Christians, Donnie was sympathetic about Amy Grant's treatment at the hands of a magazine known for its articles on counterculture personalities and rock music stars.

Donnie knew his own father had been the victim of bad press. Thus, he decided to ask Gary Chapman about the story.

"What about the *Rolling Stone* article?" Donnie questioned, after he and Glen went backstage to meet Chapman. "I know how the news media can lie about you. I'm sure it must have misquoted and misrepresented Amy."

"It was a big laugh," Chapman said smiling, "but Amy needed a little controversy to help her career."

Needless to say, Donnie was shocked by Chapman's comments. Yet in some ten minutes of conversation, he never once denied any remark made in the *Rolling Stone* interview, nor did he ever suggest she was misquoted. It seemed like a big joke more than anything else, according to Donnie.

Of course, Chapman has a habit of shocking people. When he and Amy Grant appeared on the ABC-TV program, "Good Morning, America," he was asked by hostess Joan Lunden, "What is married life with Amy really like?"

According to *Christian Contemporary Magazine*, "the comical Chapman confessed, 'it's a living hell.'"

Donnie characterized the concert as a two-hour, high-energy, loud rock and roll show with kids dancing in the aisles. Never once was any affirmation about the Lord Jesus ever made. No testimony was ever given; no admonishment to praise the Lord offered.

"The closest the concert got to anything spiritual," Donnie said later, "was Amy took about ten minutes and talked about how she's doing new things and needs our prayers."

But he also recalled during one of her heavy-rocking, strutting songs, her guitar player "stalked" her across the stage as she sang. The song closed with them back-to-back, bodies touching in movement. A lot of church kids were in attendance at the concert — some of which walked out confused at the sensual presentation they had just witnessed.

The show's opening act was singer Philip Bailey, for-merly with the pop/jazz group, "Earth, Wind, and Fire." Bailey, who professes to be born again, has recorded both Christian and secular albums recently.

About a month before the Baton Rouge concert, Bailey had the nation's number one song, "Easy Lover," written for him and co-sung with rock star Phil Collins. The song has been accused of promoting promiscuity. It was sung at the Baton Rouge concert promoted as a Christian event and supported by a number of churches.

No Stranger to Frank Comments

Amy Grant is no stranger to making frank comments or receiving criticism for her sensual, sometimes confusing, appearance. For instance, at the Grammy Awards in 1985, she wore a hand-painted, leopard spot dinner jacket and was barefooted.

However, the book, *The Heart of Rock and Roll,* included a story about her frank comments at a Christian music festival:

> It was the summer of 1980 and thousands of people, mostly teenagers, were sitting in the Florida sun listening to Amy Grant. The crowd at the Christian music festival was dressed for a day of music and sun — with most people wearing some version of shorts and summer tops.
>
> Somehow the combination of heat, halter tops, and spiritual intimacy aroused the young people, setting a mood that could best be described as "sexually charged."
>
> The then-nineteen-year-old Miss Grant could feel the mood on stage and instead of ignoring it, dismissing it, or sticking to her "act," she confronted the problem head-on:
>
> "I'm not married and I'm dying to have sex too," she said. "Sometimes I think, *If the line starts here let me be the first.* But we're making a commitment here." (Italics mine.)

Christians aren't the only ones who seem concerned about images — and words — that the young singer has expressed.

Richard Harrington of the *Washington Post* said that Grant "is projecting a confusing sexy image for an avowedly spiritual singer," while the *New York Times'* John Rockwell wrote about Grant's "deliberately alluring, even sexy publicity photos, hand on thigh and jeans rolled up to mid-calf."

> "*. . . when they knew God, they glorified him not as God, neither were thankful; but became vain in their imaginations, and their foolish heart was darkened*" (Rom. 1:21).

It's a shame when the secular world recognizes what we, as Christians, are doing is wrong. It's obvious to them. Why isn't it obvious to us?

Why does the world somehow recognize that a church standard has been broken?

For centuries the church has set the standard for decency and morality. The world recognizes that standard because the church established it. Now the secular reporters watch that standard being broken by those who claim to be Christian — and even the world knows it's against the accepted norm.

James Chute in the *Milwaukee Journal* made similar observations in his August 17, 1986, Critic's Comment:

> Lyrics aside, Grant uses all the commercial weapons available, including sex, to promote her music. Maybe her come-hither look on the album cover really suggests that she wants to have you over to talk about Jesus, but who is to know until you put the record on the turntable and actually listen to the lyrics?

Even Grant's pastor, Don Finto, of the Belmont Church in Nashville, admits, "Sometimes Amy is not always wise in the way she says things. . . ."

Leslie Phillips

But Amy Grant isn't the only contemporary Christian singer who draws attention from the sexual image she projects; she's just the most visible.

USA Today, in a story headlined "Spreading a Rock and Roll Gospel," noted the following comments about a young singer from California:

> An energetic Leslie Phillips wildly on stage, shaking her long blond hair, silver chains, and occasionally revealing her tummy.

Ironically, Ms. Phillips said in a *Contemporary Christian Magazine* interview, January 1986, ". . . sexuality's a part of all of us, but I'm not trying in any way to flaunt that in concert."

That's odd because reviewers keep writing about her in this manner, ". . . a good performer and she was a sexy girl on stage."

A St. Petersburg newspaper critic described her concert performance, saying: "She sings like Pat Benatar, dances like Sheila E., and gives the gospel like Amy Grant." Pat Benatar and Sheila E. are both well-known women singers whose brand of music is rock and roll. Sheila E. has been an opening act for Prince.

Style and Appearance

The whole issue of Christian singers and musicians — either male or female — exuding sexuality in either their public remarks, recordings, or performances is antithetical to the Gospel of the Lord Jesus Christ. To be frank, it is blasphemous.

It further raises the question: Is the world leading us or are we leading the world? In fact, why are Christians even borrowing the ways of the world?

I ponder that question extensively when I consider the appearance of a heavy metal, religious rock group like Stryper. Here's how *Time* magazine described them:

> If you had to guess their name, you might think of the Devil's Disciples or the Beelzebubs. Or perhaps the Killer Bees, which is what the four young men on stage look like in their tight leather-and-spandex costumes crisscrossed with garish black and yellow stripes. Piles of makeup, spikey hair, and enough dangling chains to tie up half the elephants in Africa complete the picture of the up-to-date heavy metal rock group. Even the music, the sound of a swarm of angry insects electronically amplified several thousand times, fits the image.

Time observed that these performers are "indistinguishable — except for their lyrics — from their secular counterparts."

Yet in looking at these performers' songs, *Newsweek* magazine, in an article titled, "The New Christian Minstrels," said:

> When these performers sing about love, the lyrics are usually romantic and sometimes ambiguous. In Grant's pop song called "Open Arms," for example, she croons, "Your love has taken hold and I can't fight it," keeping it unclear whether or not the lover is Jesus.

Frankly, I don't know what subject some of these performers are singing about. It's certainly not the Gospel. Most of the lyrics are nonsensical.

"Fight On"

Newsweek's story on "The New Christian Minstrels" also contained a description of singer Tim Miner's stage performance:

> His hair is gelled up in a new-wave pompadour. A tiny silver cross dangles from one earlobe. In his gray leather jeans, tight white "muscle shirt," and oversize cotton jacket, singer Tim Miner looks every inch the rebellious rocker.

That's precisely one of the issues in this controversy — born-again, ofttimes Spirit-baptized, young people who want to look like the rebels of this world.

Why?

The *Newsweek* article further observes:

> He grabs the microphone with one hand and lifts a clenched fist. "Fight on!" he shouts to an audience of 3,000 evangelical Christians beyond the colored floodlights. "Shake it in the devil's face and say, 'Fight on!'"

I am absolutely convinced that many of the religious rockers really don't know what they are saying. Any time the so-called sacred and sexy have been mixed, that performer has been deceived by Satan. It's that simple.

But it's even worse. You shake your fist in the devil's face all you want, but unless you've got Jesus reigning in your life, you'll likely come back with no hand if you're dealing with the real enemy.

Spiritual warfare isn't waged against the devil by shouting cutesy little slogans and shaking your fist. It's done through prayer, fasting, and acting upon God's Word alone. But that's the biblical approach and few of the religious rockers seem interested in that means.

A Catholic Magazine on Rock

In a Catholic magazine, *Liguorian,* I found the following sympathetic article, "Tuning in to Christian Rock." The article stated in part:

> The truth is, the rock sound itself makes many people feel alive and in tune with the exciting drama God is designing here on planet earth. Whatever produces that feeling is a gift, whether it's a delicious pizza, a thrilling water slide, a growling and screaming amplifier. . . .
>
> If the rock sound makes you feel alive, and if you're tuned in to faith, you'll connect that feeling with God — though probably not right away. That's okay. God doesn't expect us to think of Him directly every moment we are enjoying one of His gifts. . . .
>
> Christian rock — there is such a thing. I don't mean standard "church music" played just a little faster with more of a beat. I mean *rock* — all types, from soft to heavy metal, new wave, and punk . . .
>
> Christian rock finds a home in many places. You can listen to it just as you listen to other rock — with a nice difference . . .
>
> Christian rock also makes good background sound for open time at the parish youth room . . .
>
> God gave the rock sound to you — along with every other good thing. . . .

Believe me, God did not give the rock sound to anybody. As David Wilkerson has so aptly stated: "Rock music was born in the womb of darkness and rebellion."

"Who changed the truth of God into a lie, and worshipped and served the creature more than the Creator, who is blessed for ever. Amen" (Rom. 1:25).

The introduction to the book, *The Heart of Rock and Roll*, notes that ". . . They feel God has told them that rock must roll — back into the womb of hell where it was allegedly born."

Allegedly?

There's not one question in my mind where rock was born, nor what it has done to the lives of young people who have embraced its beat and its life-style. It has ultimately destroyed them.

The World's Influence

It is clear — beyond belief — that the world's corrupting influence has taken over the field of contemporary Christian music. The devil's music — with the accompanying beat and punk rock styles — is now being performed throughout the country. At times, the performances are even in main street churches with the nodding approval of gullible pastors.

Many of the performers are carbon copies of the world — dressed in black leather with nail-studded belts and bracelets, chains, metal collars, punk hair-dos, and painted faces.

> *"Having therefore these promises, dearly beloved, let us cleanse ourselves from all filthiness of the flesh and spirit, perfecting holiness in the fear of God"* (II Cor. 7:1).

Yet all of these performers claim to be ambassadors for Jesus. Tragically, few are.

CHAPTER
SIX

WHAT'S THE MESSAGE?

T *he music's message is clear, and adding the words Jesus*
Christ to the lyrics does not make one bit of difference.
Whether a metalhead is listening to Ozzy Osbourne or
Stryper, the feeling he or she gets in his gut is one and
the same. The music inevitably overwhelms the best intentions [or in
the cast of Osbourne, reinforces the worst intentions] of the lyrics.
— James Chute in the *Milwaukee Journal*

It is abundantly clear from the messages in the music, from the statements made in print, and from the theatrics on stage that many of these religious rockers are on an *ego trip.*

That clearly seems the motive in a number of cases where the "star syndrome" has taken over. In fact, when one religious rocker was found guilty and sentenced to fifteen years in a state prison for sex crimes, it was suggested that much of the individual's problem stemmed from the fact "he was the lead singer of a rock band." That's ego?

I categorically state that the message is more money than Gospel. Especially do I find this the case in the so-called "crossover music" that moves from the gospel arena to the Top 40 charts and the rock stations.

Contemporary Christian Magazine, in reviewing Amy Grant's record *Unguarded,* concluded:

> I really think that, given half a chance, *Unguarded* will make a significant impact in the mainstream market and expose contemporary Christian music to a whole new audience. And for those who say she's selling out, it's a matter of direction. Are we in this business to stroke the body or to take the message to a dying world? With *Unguarded,* Amy Grant takes the message where it's needed most.

The reviewer was right about one thing — the album had mainstream acceptance, going gold in 45 days and platinum in 1986.

The bigger question, however, is: What is the album's message?

Amy Grant herself was quoted in *The Heart of Rock and Roll* as saying:

> . . . And kids who are trying to find out what's really happening in this life look at somebody who is presenting all the answers and they think, *"There's no search here. They're already telling me everything. There's no looking; there's no finding."* (Italics mine.)
>
> So I found that the lyrics of this new album started not saying everything. And it wasn't an effort to say, "I'm not going to say *Jesus."* But it was an effort to say, "You know what? I want to allow a little bit of mystery of God to be in this album."

Evidently there is a lot of mystery in the album to hear many believers talk.

Ms. Grant obviously plans to take her music elsewhere other than the usual concert halls where many Christian groups perform. She has stated publicly:

I aim to bridge the gap between Christian and pop.

I can inform her that the gap will never be bridged with that which is genuinely sacred and that which is tainted with the world's emphasis and touch.

> *"Be ye not unequally yoked together with unbelievers: for what fellowship hath righteousness with unrighteousness? and what communion hath light with darkness?*
>
> *"And what concord hath Christ with Belial? or what part hath he that believeth with an infidel?*
>
> *"And what agreement hath the temple of God with idols? for ye are the temple of the living God; as God hath said, I will dwell in them, and walk in them; and I will be their God, and they shall be my people.*
>
> *"Wherefore come out from among them, and be ye separate, saith the Lord, and touch not the unclean thing; and I will receive you,*
>
> *"And will be a Father unto you, and ye shall be my sons and daughters, saith the Lord Almighty"* (II Cor. 6:14-18).

Phil Driscoll, a gifted musician and singer who has constantly testified about keeping "my craft at a level that will allow me to flow with the Holy Spirit," made the following comment to *Destiny* magazine in the January/February 1987 issue:

> I no longer believe in crossover music. Every crossover thing that I see so waters down the message of the Gospel that there is no Gospel.

That expression "no Gospel" would probably best describe the crossover efforts of many in religious rock. The Gospel of Jesus Christ becomes so watered down, it literally evaporates. The result: no Gospel.

In an interview with *People* magazine in 1983, Ms. Grant said:

> It's like there's a huge mountain called the music business, and this thing next to it, a little bitty saltshaker — that's the Christian music business. My question is, how can I sing to that mountain of people out there?

The answer to that question has evidently produced some unusual opportunities. During her fall 1984 tour of the northeast, she sold out Radio City Music Hall in New York City, the Centrum in Boston, and the Spectrum in Philadelphia. More than 17,000 people showed up for her performance in Los Angeles last year.

She also played a music theater in suburban Chicago. An advertisement on the concert read, "Miller Music at Poplar Creek." A smaller headline announced, "Miller Music Played the American Way." In case that sounds like a TV beer commercial, you're right. It's the same Miller folks that produce Miller beer.

Amy Grant appeared with special guest Russ Taff.

It's the same music theater which hosts a variety of rock groups: Dire Straits, Beach Boys, Commodores, Sting, Chaka Khan, and a menagerie of others.

The Music Industry

Rich Wilkerson, an evangelist with a special ministry to young people, observed in a recent article on religious rock:

You don't have to be around religious rock stars too long before you begin hearing a key catch word: *Industry.* The religious world has an industry that makes music just like General Motors makes cars.

The religious rock stars are very concerned that they stay in touch with where the *industry* is going. They want to do what the industry wants them to do. If the industry doesn't want them to sing a certain song, they won't. If it wants them to dress a certain way, they will.

The industry features large record companies, a major religious rock magazine, and hundreds of religious rock radio stations that play the music nationwide. For many religious rock stars, the industry is god!

U.S. News & World Report headlined an August 25, 1986, article, "Gospel music rolls out of the church, onto the charts." The story noted among other things that the big-four record companies that produce almost 100 percent of religious rock "earned $86.5 million [in 1985], up from $74 million in 1984, and 20 percent of their products were sold in mainstream record stores."

I would ask if these people are attempting to expand their market into secular areas to gain converts to Jesus Christ or to enrich themselves riding the crest of a popular music trend.

U.S. News & World Report (August 25, 1986) acknowledged the religious rock trend and the growing interest from secular record companies:

> Capitol Records already distributes records by one of the Big Four companies, Sparrow, to mainstream stores and is negotiating a similar deal with another. Mainstream retailers are more willing than ever to stock CCM, observes Dennis White, the Capitol vice-president who handles CCM distribution. "It's a good trend to be in on."

The religious rockers always maintain that they are simply trying to reach people for Jesus. If that's the case, then I'd like to suggest they go totally secular and leave out their appeal to the church. Why bother with the crowd that's already saved anyway?

Of course, since 80 percent of religious rockers' income is derived through Christian bookstores, we already know the answer to that question.

It's my conviction that the religious rockers are not reaching the lost, and there is a good chance the church could be losing the "found" by bringing rock music into the sanctuary.

Rolling Stone magazine observed the following about Amy Grant:

> In 1984 alone, Grant performed to a half million fans, grossing $1.3 million; her managers predict she'll gross more than $2.5 million from concert appearances this year [1985].

Her managers were quoted as saying, "We never *played* many churches with Amy. That was the way everybody else had done it and nobody had ever made it doing it that way."

Isn't it interesting that some people consider churches as places where you *play* instead of *minister*?

> *"Love not the world, neither the things that*
> *are in the world. If any man love the world, the*
> *love of the Father is not in him"* (I John 2:15).

If money is not the factor, then why attempt this effort at bridging the so-called gap between rock and religious? What's the purpose?

If you don't present the Gospel clearly on your recordings and you don't present it in your concerts either, how are all of these unsaved people that the rockers are supposed to be reaching suddenly going to see their need for Jesus, repent of their ways, and come to Him? What avenue have you given them?

The hard truth is, you haven't given them anything, and people can't find Jesus until somebody tells them in unmistakable terms.

Rev. Bud Calvert, pastor of Fairfax Baptist Temple, assessed some of the contemporary Christian music:

> To me, Amy Grant's music is a very fleshy, sensual program of music undermining Christianity itself. She's saying the end justifies the means, that to become a Christian you have to go down to that level. Christianity is not about God going down to our level, it is about us going up to His level.
>
> I studied the lyrics of her [recent fourth consecutive Grammy-winning] *Unguarded* album and you can't get a peanut's worth of Gospel from that record. It's ungodly, it's worldly. I think she's a sincere person, but she's sincerely wrong. . . .

> *"And they that are Christ's have crucified the flesh with the affections and lusts.*
>
> *"If we live in the Spirit, let us also walk in the Spirit.*
>
> *"Let us not be desirous of vain glory, provoking one another, envying one another"* (Gal. 5:24-26).

Keith Green's Statement

Before his untimely death in a 1982 airplane crash, singer Keith Green wrote an article decrying the trend advancing in contemporary Christian music:

> Why are we so starstruck? Why do we idolize Christian singers and speakers? We go from glorifying Elton

John in the world . . . to Andre Crouch when we become Christians. It's all idolatry! Can't you see that? . . . How come no one idolizes the missionaries who give up everything and live in poverty, endangering their lives and their families . . . How come no one lifts up and exalts the ghetto and prison ministers . . . How come? Because (1) we're taught from very early on that comfort is our goal and security . . . and (2) that we should always seek for a lot of people to like us.

Who lives more comfortably and has more "fans" than the latest bright and shining gospel star? Who lives less comfortably and has less friends and supporters than selfless missionaries?

Why do you spend more money on gospel records and concerts than you give to World Vision to feed the poor, and to the missionaries your church is supporting?

Let's all repent of idolatry and seeking a comfortable, "rewarding" life while we are passing through like strangers and pilgrims in this world (Heb. 11:13). Our due service to the Lord is *"not only to believe on him, but also to suffer for his sake"* (Phil. 1:29).

The late singer's statement brings to mind the words of Colossians 3:5:

"Mortify therefore your members which are upon the earth; fornication, uncleanness, inordinate affection, evil concupiscence, and covetousness, which is idolatry."

In this passage, covetousness is called idolatry because the thing coveted becomes an idol. It actually describes the erotomania which can be common even among Christians.

Erotomania is an extravagant display of affection or idolization even to the point of mental possession of an individual.

The erotomaniac actually falls in love with a person in high social esteem or intellectual standing, such as a diplomat, a general, an actor, a rock singer, or even a brilliant preacher. This erotomania would especially affect those who "worship" rock and roll singers.

Idolatrous admiration and worship is responsible, among other things, for the present-day "swooning" and mobbing of singers, actors, and other celebrated persons for autographs, photographs, or parts of their clothing.

What About the Lyrics?

The lyrics on many so-called religious songs seem perfectly vague and meaningless. In some cases, Jesus is not mentioned at all. The emphasis now is issues of the day. All of this, of course, is done in the name of reaching people at their level without "turning them off."

James Chute of the *Milwaukee Journal* comments:

> The contemporary Christian musicians would have us believe that changing the words changes the music's very nature, as if the power of music resides in the words alone; as if music can be completely severed from its cultural and social context and suddenly take on meanings not only removed but contradictory to those contexts . . .
>
> In the struggle between the words and the music, a struggle that has existed for centuries, music most often has the upper hand. . . .
>
> The CCM movement, however, has gone far beyond a few musicians strumming guitars and singing in harmony. Tune in to any of the Christian cable programs and you won't have to wait long before some band, dressed in its best sequins and tuxedos, looking for all the world as if its last gig was at Caesar's Palace, will praise the Almighty in the same way Las Vegas praises the almighty dollar.
>
> They all make the same fatal mistake: that somehow the lyrics change the music's context, its subliminal

message. More likely, the very opposite begins to happen: the Vegas/Wayne Newton lounge-act style is sanctified through the Christian associations.

(Amy) Grant and other middle-of-the-road Christian performers are often more subtle in their invocation of the Lord's name. They are not so overt as to actually mention the Lord; this might turn off a large segment of the mass audience they are trying to reach. So they sing about you — you as in, "You Light Up My Life." All the listener has to fill in is the blank: You can be God, but it can also be a lover, a husband, or a wife, a father or a mother, a dog or a cat.

Yet there are a few singers who do not employ this kind of approach. Dallas Holm, who has written such classics as "Rise Again" and "I Saw the Lord," is one such individual. In a March 1986 interview with *Contemporary Christian Magazine,* he talked about the potential for reaching people — yet his emphasis is considerably different from what is being expressed in many places.

> . . . If, in a concert or through my album, I can challenge Christians to be motivated to a new intensity in their walk with the Lord, they're going to, in turn, affect other lives that I would never even get to. So the potential to reach the unsaved is still greater if I can really challenge and affect the life of a believer who may be just kind of loafing.

Do you hear what he's saying? *Reach the unsaved by motivating the saved.* That's a novel approach Dallas Holm is suggesting. Why? Because the average Christian is usually kind of loafing — he or she needs desperately to be motivated! He says further:

> And so through my music — and especially on this latest album . . . I want to kind of shake American Christians to re-think what it really means to be a Christian — a

New Testament type of Christian. Radical Christianity! To re-think again the words and principles that Jesus and the Scriptures teach, to apply them literally to our lives, and to see how that stacks up against the cultural Christianity we've created.

Terry Talbot is another singer/songwriter who takes a completely different approach than what a multitude of artists are espousing today. In a February 1986 interview with *Contemporary Christian Magazine,* he said:

> The reality is that if you proclaim Jesus, the person who is seeking the Light will find it . . . It doesn't take artful lyrics and pretty songs to move someone to Jesus. There are a lot of good lyrics and pretty songs out there. It doesn't take a believer to write a great song either. It doesn't take a believer to talk about God or the Lord. It doesn't take a believer to stand against abortion or pornography. But it usually does take a believer to speak boldly and confess the name Jesus.

Talbot is right on target. How will the world ever know about the wonders of the Lord Jesus Christ unless believers tell them? How simple . . . how wonderful . . . how true!

> *"How then shall they call on him in whom they have not believed? and how shall they believe in him of whom they have not heard? and how shall they hear without a preacher?"* (Rom. 10:14).

A Shaded Opinion

Yet there are many singers, songwriters, and record companies who somehow believe there should be a totally different presentation in religious lyrics.

An article in the July 1986 issue of *Contemporary Christian Magazine* concerning a new record label — What? — explores their approach. In case you thought the name of the record company is a typographical error, the correct name is *What?* The article suggests:

> What exactly is Christian music anyway? Is it music about Christ or is it music about the entire spectrum of human existence — love, pain, relationships, death.
>
> There's been a growing contingent of artists . . . with the understanding of how to write a commercial song that could be an across-the-board hit and at the same time let out real insight into life . . . and what it means to be a human on this earth . . . tied into the Creator.
>
> The idea beyond What? is that there needed to be a place where these people could do what they do so well without being forced to fit into either of two molds. Buyers can expect releases that may be filled with biblical illusions. . . .
>
> This is material for the most part that is not about religious topics but it's made by Christians and I would hazard that's Christian music if you must define it. Literally all truth is God's truth whether or not it specifically deals with Christianity . . . what this label isn't is contemporary Christian music. The label is music done by Christians.

Do you hear what these individuals are saying? We seemingly need material with biblical illusions instead of going right to the heart of the matter and telling the wondrous old story of Jesus and His love.

Their statements are further confusing with such phrases as "all truth is God's truth whether or not it specifically deals with Christianity." We must be quick to define truth, which is actually Jesus Christ, and reality or facts. Reality may be real and facts may be true but they are not distinctly truth.

This kind of statement is frequently used in theological areas to cover up false doctrines. The realm of psychology is another prime example.

The Christian psychologist might say, "Well, admittedly, there are errors in psychology but there are also truths in psychology."

Realities or facts are being mistaken for truths. It's not a truth just because it's a reality; neither is it a truth just because it's a fact.

It is just an approach such as this that is being used to cover a mountain of error and wrongdoing in religious rock.

For instance, *Contemporary Christian Magazine* makes the following statement in its December 1986 issue:

> By providing interviews with artists and musicians, features on music-related topics, and information on records, videos, and books of particular interest to today's Christians, CCM endeavors to enhance its readers' enjoyment of, and to encourage their participation in, music which reflects a biblical perspective on all areas of life. We believe that all truth is from God and glorifies God, and that when expressed artistically, truth can be embraced by Christians regardless of the personal beliefs of the artist. Recognizing that there are many purposes for music, we focus on contemporary music which reflects biblical truth and uplifts the human spirit. . . .

Once again, reality or facts are confused with truth in this magazine's statement of purpose. The result shows a basic lack of understanding of biblical truth.

The phrase "truth can be embraced by Christians regardless of the personal beliefs of the artist" is the most dangerous statement that can be made. That's the kind of smoke screen Hitler used to cover his murderous activities against the Jews.

To suggest that an individual's life-style, pursuits, or personal beliefs do not affect what that person says has got to be one of the most incredulous statements ever made!

In effect, a truth becomes a lie basically when uttered by a liar. Thus, this person is saying, "Hey, don't do what I do; do what I say do." Of course, this is the very opposite of biblical interpretation and biblical life-style.

> *"Ye hypocrites, well did Esaias prophesy of you, saying,*
>
> *"This people draweth nigh unto me with their mouth, and honoureth me with their lips; but their heart is far from me.*
>
> *"But in vain they do worship me, teaching for doctrines the commandments of men"* (Mat. 15:7-9).
>
> *"A good tree cannot bring forth evil fruit, neither can a corrupt tree bring forth good fruit"* (Mat. 7:18).
>
> *"Many will say to me in that day, Lord, Lord, have we not prophesied in thy name? and in thy name have cast out devils? and in thy name done many wonderful works?*
>
> *"And then will I profess unto them, I never knew you: depart from me, ye that work iniquity.*
>
> *"Therefore whosoever heareth these sayings of mine, and doeth them, I will liken him unto a wise man . . ."* (Mat. 7:22-24).

CHAPTER
SEVEN

THE INFLUENCE FACTOR

 want to play hardball in this business. I want to be on the same level professionally with performers in all areas of music. I love to hear Billy Joel, Kenny Loggins, and the Doobie Brothers. Why not? I aim to bridge the gap between Christian and pop.

— Amy Grant in *Time* magazine

A youth pastor at a large Texas church drove to the metro airport to pick up a musical group who was scheduled to give a concert that night at his church.

When the group arrived and retrieved most of their equipment and luggage, the church van was loaded and the group's lead singer — a popular figure in contemporary Christian music — took the passenger seat beside the youth pastor.

The singer's first move after buckling his seat belt was to turn on the van's radio and search for the loudest, rawest rock station he could find.

Rock music with its ear-numbing, bone-crunching guitar riffs and rumbles blared throughout the church van until it arrived at the motel. All the while, the group members snapped their fingers and sang along with most of the tunes.

That, in a nutshell, portrays the influence on these religious rockers — secular rock music.

Who Influences Who?

"For it is a shame even to speak of those things which are done of them in secret" (Eph. 5:12).

Here is a record reviewer describing Stryper's newest album. Notice the language used:

Stryper combines the pinpoint harmonies of Styx with the focused guitar attack of Scorpion.

Another magazine article describes Vision's new record release:

In the early '70s, Lynyrd Skynyrd was on the cutting edge of a new breed of music. Now screaming guitars, driving rhythms, soaring electric violins, and those unmistakable keyboards make up Vision, a new band, a new sound, a new purpose.

When you read articles about these religious rockers, it might say a singer has a "Van Halen" guitar sound, or a voice like Bono of "U2", or drums that have a "Hall and Oates" sound, or music as innovative as "Duran Duran."

All of these comparisons stem from one standard line of reference: secular, gut-level, *rock and roll.*

The problem for Christians is this: If you're not aware of secular rock groups, you won't have any means of comparison to a religious rock band.

Evidently most of the magazine reviewers — even the so-called "religious publications" — assume that all Christians listen to rock music.

That is not the case!

I personally believe that many Christian young people are discerning enough to know that secular rock and roll came out of the pit of hell. Yet well-meaning, but totally misguided, individuals in religious rock have drawn many unsuspecting youngsters back to the rock and roll sound by either recording, performing, or publicizing it.

The evidence is unmistakable. The religious rockers are totally influenced by secular rock, and that clearly is reflected in the music that religious rock then creates. The result leaves the so-called contemporary Christian music reeking with the taint of the world, the rebellion of hell.

Milwaukee Journal's James Chute characterizes the music in this manner:

> For those whose eyes have not seen and whose ears have not heard, Contemporary Christian Music, or CCM as the insiders call it, is essentially conventional rock or pop music with the lyrics changed to protect the innocent.

The lyrics may have been altered, but I seriously doubt the innocent were protected.

Secular Producers

Religious rock is now big business.

Newsweek magazine reported in its August 19, 1985, edition:

> Last year [1984], for example, contemporary Christian artists sold more than 20 million albums, and this is only the top of an estimated $400 million gold mine of records, concerts, and souvenirs. . . .

Those kind of financial statistics create a considerable amount of interest in the recording industry — from record companies, producers, and musicians — all eager to jump on the newest and most popular trend.

A number of secular producers are now crossing over to produce albums in the religious rock realm. John Potoker, who produced Michael W. Smith's *The Big Picture,* which has been on the contemporary Top 10 chart for months, has also produced Mick Jagger of the Rolling Stones.

This is the same Mick Jagger who has recorded songs ranging from the espousal of violent revolution in "Street Fighting Man" to the anthem of satanists, "Sympathy for the Devil." Jagger has been dubbed "the Lucifer of rock and roll" by more than one interviewer.

In fact, one publication suggested, "With voodoo incantations and the screams of demon possession accompanying cuts like "Dancing with Mr. D" [the devil], one is left wondering if perhaps the satanic imagery of Mr. Jagger and company is all concocted."

And now one of Jagger's former producers has produced an album for Smith, who had made a name for himself writing and performing praise songs like "Hosanna," "Great Is the Lord," and "How Majestic Is Your Name." Apparently the new record represents a sharp change in direction for Smith.

A June 1986 article in *Contemporary Christian Magazine* profiling Smith and Potoker stated:

> The result of the collaboration is evident in the
> *brashness* of Michael's new songs which strike with the
> abrupt strength of an expertly snapped wet towel on a dry
> summer day. The music *unleashes a rock 'n' roll power*
> only hinted at in Michael's previous work. (Italics mine.)

Could it be that Potoker's experience with Mick Jagger
has strongly influenced Smith's album? The answer would
have to be an obvious yes.

The *CCM* story entitled "Smitty Gets Gritty" also
contained the following observation:

> In concert, Michael will sometimes jump from the
> stage to dance with the young women who have rushed the
> stage. He remembers the first time he did it. The show was
> in California, and Debbie [his wife] was backstage. The
> next night, the girls again flocked in front of him, but this
> time he didn't join them.

Isn't it ironic that an artist who is already quoted as
saying "asking for a decision" from young people "is not
my call" can still feel the liberty to jump down from the
stage and dance with young girls?

That's a measure of the wrongness of religious rock.
Where is God in such raw, worldly conduct? How is Jesus
glorified in such nonsense?

The truth is, He's not! *He is blasphemed!*

Smith and Potoker aren't the only ones, unfortunately.
There are a host of others. The producer, for instance, who
did Russ Taff's *Medals* album and Amy Grant's
Unguarded recently listed his musical influences:

> I would say the music for the Eighties in Chaka Khan's
> *Feel for You* and Hall & Oates' *Big Bam Boom* are definite
> examples of modern music. I like songs on the Top 40
> format.

That individual's statement clearly shows the influence on his music which, of course, is reflected in the music he will then produce for others. Hence, the religious rock sound is no different from its secular rock brother.

The hard cold fact is, there is no difference.

Double-Talk

"But I have a few things against thee, because thou hast there them that hold the doctrine of Balaam, who taught Balac to cast a stumblingblock before the children of Israel, to eat things sacrificed unto idols, and to commit fornication" (Rev. 2:14).

New bands appear to be the order of the day. Undercover is one such group which favors the "new wave" sound. A promotional flyer describes the band:

> Blue Collar is pleased to present *Branded*, the long-awaited fourth album from Undercover. Undercover's raw emotion and driving music has won them a large following throughout the U.S. and Europe. *Branded* combines a maturing of the band's intense rock with deeply moving lyrics that make *Branded* a very important album.

Sometimes it's difficult to discern much about a group from simply listening to their music. In Undercover's case, the music is pretty raw and definitely from the "new wave" school of rock and roll.

However, most of the religious rockers are frequently quoted. Undercover's Joey Taylor of the California-based group made the following statements to the *San Diego Union:*

> I'm not connected with Christian music at all. I can't
> stand Christian radio stations, and Christian TV makes me
> want to barf. Our music is a vehicle for our Christianity.

Describing Undercover with "punk looks and ragged
rock sounds," *What About Christian Rock* quotes Taylor:

> Our desire is to be credible to these kids, who, even
> though they are not violent, rebellious, satanic, punk
> rockers, they enjoy this style of music. We can reach them
> that way. But we also feel led to call, reach out to those
> people who are extremely violent. . . .

It sounds like Joey, who sports a modified mohawk
haircut and wears chains and leather, is giving us some
double-talk which seems fairly typical for most of the
religious rockers. I have felt they contradict almost everything they say with conflicting statements, their style of
dress, or their music.

The groups who are coming onto the scene now apparently have decided *they* will set the standard for music.
They'll play what they please and nobody will tell them
differently.

Of course, that is the spirit of the world — rebellion. It
came into the world with Satan's act of rebellion against
God and is now manifest in a number of ways within
religious rock. It is still the spirit of lawlessness.

Bash-N-The Code

Here is an album review for a group called Bash-N-The
Code, which someone suggested has an "androgynous
look" in its appearance:

> They debut a brainstormer of a debut album . . . what
> keeps the Bash from dance mania is a stunning rock guitar

solo obviously influenced by Eric Clapton and Jeff Beck. He adds a certain music style to tunes the dance floor often neglects. . . .

This album review, from *Contemporary Christian Magazine,* gives the basic direction this group is headed with its music — the dance floor.

Is that what music which supposedly relates to God Almighty should be doing? Or does it really matter anymore?

The very title of the group, Bash-N-The Code, is an attack against traditional Christianity. In essence, the group's title is suggesting, *"We don't believe in these 'thou shalt nots' of the Ten Commandments and of Christianity as a whole. By our life-style, our actions, and our group name, we're saying do away with most of that old-fashioned stuff."*

Once you get down to the basic premise with these groups, they are suggesting, "Do away with most of the Bible. We have little interest in Bible Christianity. We will have our own type of Christianity."

> *"If the foundations be destroyed, what can the righteous do?"* (Psa. 11:3).

Another new group is called Stricken. A review stated "the group is visibly more shocking than Motley Crue. The foursome sports on-stage armor and new music they call thunder rock."

Youth Choir, a popular group at Christian festivals, changed its name recently to The Choir. A recent album review on the band stated:

> Daugherty's uniquely arresting guitar sounds are driven to new heights of expression by the propulsive, drum attack. Songs move from a police-like attack . . . guitar riffs to a full throttle rock with a hot sax. Youth

Choir softens the new music palet, prodding the con-
science.

Do you sense anything with these record reviews that
bespeak of faith towards God, holiness, or any of the fruit
of the Spirit which the Bible admonishes us to reflect? Do
you find anything edifying or encouraging in these music
reviews about the Lord Jesus Christ *directly?*

I don't; I only find sacrilege.

Yet the groups persist in their outrageous comments.
According to Derald Daugherty, The Choir's guitarist/
vocalist:

The music is basically a cultural thing. And God can
use anything. We have chosen this kind of music as a
vehicle for God.

Festivals and The Grateful Dead

It seems ironic there could be any real link between the
acid rock group, The Grateful Dead, and Christian music
festivals, but that's exactly what writer Brian Quincy Newcomb suggested in the July/August 1986 issue of *Contemporary Christian Magazine*.

Writing about the festivals where there is "plenty of
rock 'n' roll," the article made frequent reference to the
music events and the rock group. Newcomb concluded by
saying:

Folks who listen to the Dead don't listen because the
band members are great musicians. Often they aren't. They
don't listen to the Dead because they're innovative.
They've been doing essentially the same thing for nearly
20 years. People listen to the Dead because they like how
the music feels, they like the atmosphere around the
music, and they enjoy the other folks who enjoy the Dead.

Such comparisons might seem perfectly innocent and harmless unless you know something about the history of the Grateful Dead. According to the book, *Why Knock Rock?*

> The Grateful Dead . . . spokesman and "resident guru," Jerry Garcia, described the group's popular sound, acid rock, as "music you listen to when you are high on acid." The Dead was known as the band that stood for rebellion and drugs, and its fans were heavy dopers. A typical concert was often sotted with LSD as well as pot, and Dead's followers have appropriately been dubbed "dead-heads." Describing a Dead concert, an article in *Us* magazine stated, "Wine-filled goatskins, marijuana, and assorted other 'party favors' are passed through the crowd."

Newcomb's article on the music festivals also noted the fact that one band, "Adam Again — the newest band on Blue Collar Records — dressed in Salvation Army and Goodwill specials."

Under a photograph of the group, the cutline read: "New music band Adam Again teaches Midwesterners the meaning of 'boogie.'"

I don't know what any of this nonsense has to do with the Gospel of the Lord Jesus Christ.

To be frank with you, to compare some type of Christian endeavor with the basest of rock groups (or any rock group at all) is little more than blasphemy. The very idea that any comparison could be offered shows the absolute degeneracy of the individuals connected with the religious rock scene.

People who flock to these events, performers who play them, magazines who write about them, and pastors who give their seal of approval to them either have little knowledge of the Word of God, or are very shallow in their Christianity, *or else they are close to being reprobates.*

*"Who knowing the judgment of God, that
they which commit such things are worthy of
death, not only do the same, but have pleasure in
them that do them"* (Rom. 1:32).

Does Integrity Matter?

It is clear — even though this sub-heading has been
titled "Does Integrity matter?" — that actually linking
integrity with religious rock is like comparing Mary, the
mother of our Lord, with a common prostitute on the street.

Anyone who would try to do such — as we have seen in
this book's pages — would be misguided at least and
absolutely ludicrous at worst.

Some years ago the late Keith Green was quoted as
saying:

> I do believe that the Holy Spirit is grieved by a lot of
> what is being passed today as music ministry and gospel
> music — not so much by the beat or content, but by the
> lack of commitment and anointing.

In an article published in *Destiny* magazine (May/June
1986 issue) on "Today's Music," Larry Tomczak made
some of the same observations:

> . . . Over my past fifteen years in ministry, I have
> made many friends in the music field, sitting face to face
> and sharing honest fellowship at Jesus festivals, con-
> ferences, and concerts throughout this country. At times I
> have been grieved by what I've seen. I do not speak
> harshly or by way of hearsay, as I have been privileged to
> minister with many artists during 31 Jesus festivals dating
> back to the very first one in 1973.
>
> I've repeatedly seen musicians ministering out of an
> "empty well," confessing to me that their own spiritual
> life was almost nonexistent, having been swallowed up by

> the demands of the touring "circuit" as they try to get to
> the top.
>
> . . . How many of these artists, and others like them,
> have compulsive eating and drinking problems, offer shal-
> low presentations of the gospel, persistently battle with
> immorality, and exhibit a seemingly complete lack of
> vision for what God is currently doing on the earth — all
> stemming from a lack of a dynamic, ongoing personal
> relationship with Jesus Christ?

Evidently integrity is not even the question — since
few of the individuals involved in religious rock seem to
have any.

Album Reviews of Secular Artists

To give you an idea how far religious rock is slipping
from its biblical moorings, consider the fact that *Contemporary Christian Magazine* recently carried album reviews
on two well-known pop artists, Stevie Wonder and Jackson
Browne.

Wonder, who has made hit records since he was eight
years old, had a big hit this past year with a song entitled,
"Part-Time Lover."

His latest album was called "a state of the art delight"
by the magazine reviewer.

The review on Jackson Browne pontificated:

> Apparently religion is important to Jackson Browne,
> but he is yet to find a way to make it relevant to his own life.

After making that incredible statement, the magazine
writer then suggested in an unbelievable fashion:

> We would be right to give Jackson Browne a listen to
> see if there isn't something we can learn from what he says.

Why should anybody listen to Jackson Browne? Especially any born-again child of God?

What are you going to learn from somebody who is searching for the answers we have already found in Jesus Christ?

Why should I go to a searcher when I've got God's Word that provides the answers?

This is utter nonsense!

The problem with all of this is the blending of the holy and the unholy. It is a complete violation of Ezekiel 44:23, *"And they shall teach my people the difference between the holy and profane."*

Performers tour from city to city giving a secular concert in one place and a religious one in another. Record producers ply their production artistry for the Rolling Stones' Mick Jagger as well as the latest Christian star — seemingly without a problem.

Religious magazines review secular artists in the same breath with religious ones and blindly suggest we should listen to them . . . and readers, who claim Christ as Saviour and should know better, will follow that kind of ignorant advice.

Jesus declared:

> *"No man can serve two masters"* (Mat. 6:24).

Yet after two thousand years, people still try.

> *"Let them alone: they be blind leaders of the blind. And if the blind lead the blind, both shall fall into the ditch"* (Mat. 15:14).

HEAVY METAL MISSIONARIES?

he hair is long and the screams are loud 'n' clear. The clothes are tight, earrings dangling from their ears. No matter how we look, we'll always praise His name. And, if you believe, you've got to do the same.
— Stryper from *Loud 'n' Clear*

The most controversial band in contemporary Christian music — without question — is Stryper, whose unorthodox appearance and music have come to symbolize much of what is wrong with religious rock.

Even religious rock's bible, *Contemporary Christian Magazine,* offered this startling comment about the California foursome in its December 1986 issue:

To be completely honest, our criticism of Stryper has had more to do with doctrine than method . . . We think Stryper's lyrics have at times reflected a view of God that is shallow, overly simplistic, and (arguably) unscriptural. . . .

97

Stryper's lead vocalist and guitarist, Michael Sweet, even seems to distance the group from other religious rockers in *What About Christian Rock?* He said Stryper performs:

> . . . more of a mainstream-type music with a Christian message. We try to stay away from a title like "contemporary Christian music" because we really don't seem to be that . . . But we find that when people classify us as contemporary Christian artists, it actually takes away from what we're trying to achieve.

James Chute of the *Milwaukee Journal* — in an article entitled, "What hath pop wrought in Jesus' name?" — said:

> Stryper offers the most extreme example. Clad in black and yellow leather and spandex costumes complete with the mandatory chains, leather bracelets, spiked hair, and makeup, Stryper claims to play its ear-shattering, mind-numbing heavy metal rock for Jesus.

In a *Time* magazine profile of religious rock entitled, "New Lyrics for the Devil's Music," the article (March 11, 1985, edition) opened with a verbal picture of Stryper:

> The group is actually called Stryper, a name inspired by the biblical assurance that *"with His stripes we are healed"* (Isaiah 53:5) . . . "We are rock 'n' roll evangelists," says drummer Robert Sweet, 24. "Stryper is a modern-day John the Baptist crying in the world of rock for those who don't have the life of Christ to turn on the light switch. Our message is J-E-S-U-S."

The Roxx Regime

According to published reports, Robert and Michael Sweet, along with the rest of their family, accepted Christ in

1975 because of a Jimmy Swaggart telecast. The brothers apparently had a strong interest in music. Thus, they placed the Lord on the back burner and concentrated on rock and roll.

They had put together a secular rock and roll band from Los Angeles known as the Roxx Regime, trying to make it to the top among several hundred bands in the expanse known as Southern California.

Then a musician friend, Ken Metcalf, suggested, "If you change your group around and glorify Jesus, you'll go straight to the top."

As the story goes, the band rededicated their lives to the Lord, changed their name to Stryper, and took a demo tape to Los Angeles-based Enigma Records, the same company that launched two other heavy metal bands, Ratt and Motley Crue.

The group's first album, *The Yellow and Black Attack*, was named for the band's colors. That was followed by *Soldiers Under Command,* released in 1985, which reportedly sold 350,000 units internationally, stayed over 40 weeks on *Billboard's* Top 200 album chart and over a year on the magazine's inspirational chart.

Stryper's third album, *To Hell with the Devil,* according to published reports (*CCM,* December 1986), was released in the fall of 1986 with advance orders of 350,000 units.

The Stryper Sound

James Chute characterizes Stryper's heavy metal sound as an "orchestra of jackhammers." Rock historian Lester Bangs, in considering the roots and context of heavy metal rock, says:

> Of all contemporary rock, it is the genre most closely identified with violence and aggression, rapine and carnage.

Heavy metal orchestrates technological nihilism . . . it's a fast train to nowhere, which may be one reason it seems to feel so good and make so much sense to its fans.

Its noise is created by electric guitars, filtered through an array of warping devices from fuzztone to wah-wah, cranked several decibels past the pain threshold, loud enough to rebound off the walls of the biggest arenas anywhere. Add the aural image of a battering ram, and you've got a pretty good picture of what heavy metal sounds like.

The Heart of Rock and Roll generously looks at Stryper's music in a totally different perspective:

. . . There's more than raw, untrained power. There's finesse. The members of Stryper are arguably better musicians than members of Ratt, Motley Crue, Iron Maiden, and other bands who confuse volume with musical power, screaming with singing, and bombast with truth.

Vocalist Michael Sweet wraps his vocal chords around a handful of octaves and styles . . . Sweet takes command of the stage, giving an energetic performance that is masculine but not erotic.

And he plays a mean guitar, too.

Brother Robert . . . sitting in a drum chair with "Jesus Christ Rocks" printed on the back . . . makes his drum set talk, punctuating the band's songs with a pounding bass drum, crashing cymbals, and fluid solos.

Oz Fox leads the guitar assault, tossing his head and curly long black hair as he stabs the air with stratospheric lead guitar breaks. And bassist Tim Gaines gives the music a bottom, adding background vocals to the mix.

As with all the religious rockers, the standard of comparison with Stryper is with the secular rock artists. That's the constant connection. Robert Sweet has said his goal has been to play drums like Eddie Van Halen plays guitar.

Michael Sweet says his musical influences were Lionel Ritchie and Boz Scaggs. He also likes the group, Survivor. "Their songs are put together so well," he says.

The secular musical influence — obviously the dominate heavy metal touch — conditions the sound and stage performance Stryper gives.

Pat Boone's Comments

Pat Boone, who was first drawn into the spotlight in the 1950s pop music scene, is now hosting a so-called religious music video show. The singer, known for his "white buck" shoes and glass of milk, offers this comment about bands like Stryper:

> . . . are speaking the kids' language, but they are getting a different message than they are hearing from W.A.S.P. . . . or Motley Crue, or all these other groups that sing about sadomasochism and bestiality and drugs and suicide and actual satanism . . . Kids understand that message.

Michael Sweet seems to echo Pat Boone's comment when he says:

> We're trying to attract non-Christian audiences. We want kids who are into AC/DC or Motley Crue to be able to proudly say, "Look, maybe I'm not a Christian yet, but I'm going to see Stryper." Christians have to understand, there are a lot of kids out there who need to be reached who aren't going to be reached by the way they do it. . . .

The big question is, are they being reached?

The answer is a resounding *no* according to Andy Secher in an article, "Stryper, Angels with Dirty Faces," in the January 1987 issue of *Hit Parader* magazine. (*Hit*

Parader is one of the most vile teen rock magazines in the country, little more than rock and roll pornography.) The article stated:

> While Sweet and the rest of Stryper are not about to admit it, *apparently a majority of the band's fans have little or no idea about the group's spiritual message.* A survey held at a recent Stryper show indicated that, while 90 percent of the crowd was extremely pleased by the group's onstage preformance, *less than half were even remotely aware of the group's religious stance. . . .* (Italics mine.)

What Overpowers the Message?

If Secher's survey is correct and I have no reason to dispute it, what could possibly be hindering Stryper's audience from understanding their message?

Could it be the decibel level of their sound? Could their costumes and stage antics be a factor?

I believe both are prime candidates.

The group's (typical) sound is loud almost beyond belief. One reviewer suggested during a Texas concert that the band could probably be heard "at least two miles away."

James Chute suggests:

> Go to a concert by Judas Priest, Iron Maiden, or any other metal band and you might be able to understand a word here or there, but not many. Maybe some of the metal aficionados have all the words memorized, but don't bet on it. The words don't really matter because *the message is in the music."* (Italics mine.)

Hit Parader quotes Robert Sweet as saying:

> We know there are plenty of people who question what
> we're doing because of the way we look and the way we act
> onstage . . . we are a rock and roll band. We grew up on
> KISS, Van Halen, and Deep Purple. So we see nothing
> wrong with looking good onstage and playing with power.
> After all, God is entitled to only the best — so why not
> celebrate His name with the best type of music in the
> world?

This statement, "looking good onstage and playing
with power," needs to be qualified. Looking good to
whom? And playing with what kind of power?

Does Stryper look good to God? If the group looks
good to *Hit Parader,* it is very doubtful they could look
good to God. If the group was playing with Holy Ghost
power, it's obvious *Hit Parader* would not feature them. If
they did, it would no doubt be a caustic review if they got
one at all.

So the answer to why Stryper plays so loud is: *We* grew
up with this kind of music and *we* don't see anything wrong
with it. In other words, *we set the standards.*

What about the justification for the garish yellow and
black spandex leather clothes? Michael Sweet is quoted in
the book, *What About Gospel Rock?*

> In no way do I want to be sexually explicit, but all
> you've got to do is compare us with those [secular] rock
> bands of today. Does Stryper have the seat of their pants
> cut out [as David Lee Roth has done]? Is Stryper sticking
> something in their pants to draw attention [as nearly every
> metal band has done at one time or another]?

The book then pontificates:

> Sweet does have a point: compared to other secular
> heavy metal groups, Stryper is very mild in appearance.
> Their stage presentation — when we viewed it — didn't

employ the crowd-enticing, sexually-suggestive posturing of most secular heavy metal concerts. And their LP covers and videos, though brash, have no sexual connotations.

It seems the sole basis for justifying a group like Stryper — and countless others — is the "comparison test." The comparison is always with secular rock.

That's the problem.

The Lord tells us the world is our enemy. For them to set a standard based on what the world does lets a person know these groups don't even know what the standard is.

The standard is not set by the secular rock artists. The correct standard is set by the Word of God. This standard is molded into our lives by the Holy Spirit, God's special instrument. Evidently none of the religious rockers desire to have this standard established for them by the Holy Spirit.

It's always a comparison test with the world — "ours is not as bad as theirs." It reminds me of the two drunks arguing. "I'm not as drunk as you are" was the heart of the fight.

Christianity Today's Article

When *Christianity Today* printed a profile of Stryper, the evangelical magazine received a number of letters from readers. The letters asked questions which cry out to be answered:

> • Is not the mixing of Christian and heavy metal a contradiction in contrasting ideologies? If we were to evangelize prostitutes, would we be expected to dress like them also?
> • Our missionaries bringing the Gospel to the world do not dress as witch doctors to convert the natives.
> • An article about a Christian heavy metal band is the

same as writing about a 'Christian' physician who performs abortions and says he makes an impact on the murderers of America who also perform abortions.

A Money-Making Gimmick?

Is the entire idea of a heavy metal band like Stryper — with spandex and leather outfits and long spikey hair — nothing more than a money-making scheme?

That's the question the *Hit Parader* article pondered:

> Listening to Sweet's thoughtfully presented dialogue, one can't help but be impressed by Stryper's dedication and creativity. Still, the idea that the band's unique presentation is little more than a money-making gimmick — much like the celebrated exploits of the Crue or Ozzy — can't be easily dismissed. . . .

That question about money-making gimmicks also can be raised from Robert Sweet's comments to *Hit Parader:*

> . . . We wanted to combine our two great passions — Jesus and rock and roll — and so far we've been quite successful. The message is always there, but we're good enough musically for even non-religious people to get into what we're playing. That's the big advantage we have over a band like Motley Crue. We can appeal to their audience, but we also have the spiritual people behind us — at least most of 'em. There are 100 million Christians in the United States. If even a small segment of those people get into what we're doing, we'll be very successful.

It seems the question which should be raised is, "What constitutes success in the religious rock realm?"

That answer seems obvious. Money is the core of all efforts. You can add to that the recognition factor or "ego" and the acceptance by the world. Then it's regarded as a success. If Stryper and other religious rock groups can get Motley Crue's audience to like them, then they can label themselves successful.

It's obvious what these groups are doing. They really have no concern for God or His ways. Everything they do could be labeled little more than blasphemy — absolute, utter blasphemy. What they are attempting is to capture that place in the market created by the excesses of the secular rock groups.

The secular rock groups have become so dirty, so satanic, so degrading, that they have "turned off" an entire segment of the population.

So along comes other rock and roll bands who call themselves "Christian." The very word itself calms the fears of concerned parents. It's "Christian" so it has to be all right. It's something the kids can follow without being destroyed through drug addiction, illicit sex, or Satan worship.

And the religious rock bands capitalize on that parental fear. Their outlandish clothes will be similar to the world's. The strobe lights, the smoke bombs, and the sound itself will be like the secular groups. The only difference will be in the words and the toned-down gestures onstage. The religious rockers have now justified their actions — and, besides, they're making good money at it as well. They are now successful.

Only in God's eyes they are anything *but* successful!

CHAPTER
NINE

THE
SUPERSTARS

or what it's worth, Amy Grant is a bonafide star.
— *Contemporary Christian Magazine* cover story

Just as the secular rock world has its superstars — Bruce Springsteen, Michael Jackson, Paul McCartney, and others — so does religious rock. Who are these individuals and what are they saying to us? I have arbitrarily chosen six — three men, two groups, and one woman — to give a preview of the direction, influence, and musical styles of the music's leaders.

Even though the religious rock has its superstars — a situation which can occur in the ministry also — the very idea of such is foreign to biblical Christianity. Once again, it is an oxymoron, an impossibility of the melding of light and darkness.

The superstar concept, whether in the ministry or religious rock, has its birth in the pit. It was that same deadly force which threatened to destroy the fledgling group of disciples even in the very midst of the Lord's earthly ministry.

> *"And there was also a strife among them, which of them should be accounted the greatest.*
> *"And he said unto them, The kings of the Gentiles exercise lordship over them; and they that exercise authority upon them are called benefactors.*
> *"But ye shall not be so . . ."* (Luke 22:24-26).

The cause of Satan's downfall was that he desired to be God. That spirit pervades the world today, causing the greater part of man's inhumanity to man. Really, it should be a tip-off that "something is wrong" when superstars are spawned not only in religious rock but in southern gospel as well, and, I might add, in the ministry — where it will destroy an individual quicker than anything else.

Leon Patillo

Leon Patillo was lead singer and keyboard player for four years (1973-1977) for the secular rock group Santana — known for its songs like "Black Magic Woman" and others. In the last several years he has become increasingly popular within religious rock with the same style of music — a wedding of pop/rhythm and blues with religious lyrics.

Yet his career, even within the religious realm, has created a controversial stir according to *Contemporary Christian Magazine:*

> Last year [1984], Leon went out on tour with a set of sequencers as a one-man show. This year [1985], he's

going out with a band — the members of which are all white, all female, and all unsaved.

The flack is already starting to come in. One "know-it-all" even complained that Leon was trying to become "the Christian Prince." But the singer feels quite strongly about the lineup for two reasons.

First, Leon felt led to hire non-Christians based on a very early example. "I really prayed about it and said, 'Lord, am I going the right route with this sort of thinking?'

"He said, 'Well, all you have to do is check Me out. I did the same thing when I was going out to get My disciples. I went out and caught a couple of fishermen and said, "I'm going to make you fishers of men."

Of course, He could say that. But the point is that He didn't run down to the local synagogue and try to get a group together. He went out into the streets . . .

"I really believe that, as Christians, we should be the first to do something," Leon enthuses. "We should let the world copy *us*. They come with "We are the World," so we go and get all the Christians together and sing a song. We should be setting the pace, because we're serving the God of all creativity — and we all know how wild God's imagination is.

"I'm going to make a stand. I'm going to do some-thing different. I'm going to let the world stand up and say, 'Wow, man, did you see that guy?' And it's going to be a perfect setup. As soon as they've got their mouths open or their hearts open and they're going 'Wow,' I'm gonna throw Jesus right down their throats."

The overpowering problem I have with Leon's remarks is his terrible misconception about the men Jesus called. First, they were men, not women. And these men (Peter, James, John, etc.) in today's vernacular would be consid-ered mature Christians even before they stepped out to follow the Lord. So to suggest the analogy that Jesus did not go into the synagogue but went to the streets instead has absolutely *no basis* in Scripture or comparison in fact regarding those men He chose to follow Him.

All of these men were staunch believers in the Old Covenant (which is all they had at that time). They were mature in their development — some having been followers of John the Baptist.

However, to equate the disciples of Jesus with the unsaved members of a religious rock band borders on blasphemy or a total lack of knowledge of the Word of God — I suspect the latter case being the true problem.

This is the kind of muddled theology which pervades much of religious rock and its performers. Yet these people are hailed as spiritual leaders to millions of young people. The saddest part is, many gullible Christians buy their message without knowing the scriptural truth.

Like many of the religious rockers who have aspirations of a broader marketplace, the article quotes Patillo as looking toward an impact on that general market. "I get a chance to do a secular concert every once in a while," he is quoted as saying.

Sound familiar? It's a frequent refrain with most of the religious rockers. No doubt most of them have never considered this scriptural application to their lives:

> "Thou therefore endure hardness, as a good soldier of Jesus Christ.
> "No man that warreth entangleth himself with the affairs of this life; that he may please him who hath chosen him to be a soldier.
> "And if a man also strive for masteries, yet is he not crowned, except he strive lawfully"
> (II Tim. 2:3-5).

Philip Bailey, formerly with the soul/pop group, Earth, Wind, and Fire, credits Leon Patillo with being instrumental in his full-on commitment to Christ. Bailey also stated one of the reasons he stayed in secular music:

When people talk to us about how I can be in secular music, my biggest example was Leon being in Santana. That's how I cut my teeth. I see it as being such an effective tool, unless the Lord has told you differently.

Steve Taylor

The son of a Baptist pastor in Denver and a former youth minister himself, the *Los Angeles Times* says "rock 'n' roller Steve Taylor breaks tradition with a sledgehammer."

Billboard magazine stated, "Steve Taylor has an edge and vitality rare for any act."

The book, *The Heart of Rock and Roll*, attempts to describe Steve Taylor's music in the following way:

. . . Music that is riddled with satire, quirky, tinged with more than a hint of new wave rock, and anything but comforting?

Watch out when Taylor sets his sights on some of our most revered Christian leaders. He calls them "brylcreem prophets" or "charlatans in leisure suits," and pokes holes in their teachings.

And Taylor doesn't write about familiar places found in Christian vacation guides. He takes us to Madame Tussaud's famed wax museum in London (which serves as an illustration of hell and judgment) and to the Reptile Gardens Curio Shop, a place located nowhere but in the songwriter's own fertile imagination.

He sings about spiritual battles, some of which even angels have not yet dared to view (like the duel with the devil in the backseat of a Chevy).

And his characters aren't all noble and virtuous. No, they try to get by with everything: marital infidelity, hypocrisy, abortion, suicide, and insanity. But they rarely succeed.

Even the religious folk that populate Taylor's songs have their faults. In fact, Taylor's three recordings present a

virtual catalog of the ills and idiosyncrasies of the modern
American church — everything from country-club Christianity, through church-supported racism, to spiritual
pride.

How does Taylor view gospel music? Here's a quote
from an interview published in February 1986's edition of
Contemporary Christian Magazine:

> I appeared on the Dove Awards last year and I still feel
> uncomfortable about it. I really don't belong there because
> I'm not really part of that Gospel mainstream. Sure, I'm a
> Christian and that influences the way I write songs but
> that's just being honest, everybody pushes a point of view.
> Is Madonna's music just for whores? Is Prince's music just
> for sexual deviates? Christian musicians should be less
> concerned about being accepted with their peers and work
> on saying something different.

What these people are actually saying is this: The Bible
is outdated and old-fashioned. It doesn't apply to *modern*
life. We have a better way of doing things — *our* way.

Once again, this isn't new. It's an old story begun in the
Garden of Eden and repeated ever since. Religious rockers
have simply restated it — another type of Christianity, yet
it has no basis in the Bible.

But let me tell you, the Bible is for every age group and
for every age. It doesn't matter how old you get, just say it
the way it is. There won't be another instruction book
given. The same word Moses gave to Pharaoh is the same
word you can give to the modern-day monarchs of Egypt.

Taylor is further quoted as saying:

> I've got to say that when my songs started drawing fire
> because they were too controversial, I knew I was on the
> right track. Everything I do I sort of stumble into, and that
> gives me the freedom to stumble into anything.

Assessing Taylor's musical contributions, another article noted:

> Extensive touring last year [1985] with Sheila Walsh in Europe and the U.S. confirmed his reputation as a powerful new arrival on the scene. His edgy, punk-influenced sound matched perfectly the cutting insights and brittle sense of irony that set his music apart from the often rote retreads of much of the rank and file.

Taylor made a video entitled "Lifeboat" in which he dressed as a woman teaching an elementary school class on values clarification. Then all of the kids throw him out the window while singing, "seeing if the teacher can bounce."

There is no substance to such videos — no Jesus, no God, no nothing.

Perhaps it could be correctly termed a religious nihilism — characterized by no future, no substance, no hope. Rock music authority Lester Bangs has said the sound is "a fast train to nowhere" and that quality is evident in secular rock's offspring, religious rock and roll.

Religious rock does not offer hope. Since it is Spiritless, it can give none. It does not offer heaven, for the music within itself produces a vacuum — full of sound and fury but no substance. It provides no foundation to the believer because its birth came from secular rock and roll which has no basis in God.

Mylon LeFevre

Like many other religious rockers, Mylon LeFevre is making some radical changes with his approach — but I am as troubled about his old methods as I am with his new ones.

An interview Mylon gave *Christian Contemporary Magazine* (March 1986), contained the following remarks:

> If the critics are upset now, Mylon thinks they'll have a field day in the not-too-distant future. . . .
>
> One of the things Mylon may be referring to is a new album due out soon from CBS. He and the band are going by the name, Look Up. "It's a Christian album, but you really have to know the Word to know it. CBS ain't gonna know it. Every song on there — every note on there — is played by born-again, Spirit-filled Christians. We had a good time making the record. It's an anointed record and it's got a good message, but it's very shallow. We really avoided certain words and phrases, you know. It's just about themes.

I have a very hard time accepting his statement **equat-**ing *anything* anointed with being shallow. In over **thirty** years of full-time ministry, I have seen the anointing of God set the captives free. It break bondages over people. Every problem in life can be solved under the anointing of the Holy Spirit of God.

The article continues:

> Uh-h. Is Mylon selling out? He doesn't think so. "I wouldn't go into a situation where I had to compromise what I've been called to do. If I can't teach and preach and make disciples exactly the way I do now, if going and getting on tour with somebody who would want me to water it down."

I'm not sure what Mylon's telling us. First, he states that he's recorded a secular album for a secular company and dropped all the references to Jesus. Then he says he won't compromise or water down things. It seems pretty obvious he has.

Since the "music is the message," I'm not sure any-body who follows Mylon will know the difference — or care.

The article further quoted Mylon as saying:

> We considered doing a couple of tours, like maybe opening for Eric Clapton. We wouldn't go out with some metal band or something, but if it were somebody who draws a mellow audience like Eric, what I would do with that opportunity is to tell them exactly the same thing I do now. I wouldn't change. I wouldn't compromise teaching and preaching and making disciples for any amount of money.

If Mylon took such a step — going on tour with a famed rock performer like Eric Clapton — how would he expect to get his message across in an arena filled with thousands of people, marijuana smoke blowing under his nose, and stoned or drunk individuals screaming for songs about drugs, sex, and satanism?

How can *anybody* get his message across in such a scene?

> Nonetheless, in making an album for the pop market, Mylon set out to work on some general songs that wouldn't have direct or even subtle spiritual messages, but a problem developed. "I went to write this album, and I was going to write some secular-type tunes. I'm not opposed to that. If you're a plumber, you plumb. If you're a mechanic who gets born again, you still work on cars, not just on Christian cars. I just didn't enjoy it. I couldn't do it, but creating is fun when you're doing what means something to you. If not, you're prostituting your art. . . .

When a man who has written plenty of rock and roll songs in the past suddenly could not produce one, as Mylon described, I wondered if the Holy Spirit was dealing with him not to write such songs. That seemed obvious to me. Yet when he couldn't write the tunes, he simply got songs from others. Here's an example, in Mylon's own words, of one of the songs:

> A couple of songs don't have any message . . . There's
> one that Dana Key wrote about an old relationship. A girl
> walked out on him. He just dragged this sucker out of the
> closet and dusted it off, and it was a good rock 'n' roll
> song. It ain't got nothing to do with Jesus. It's just a song
> and we recorded it.

Honestly, I don't understand the logic in any of these comments. I feel buried in a sea of contradictions.

Mylon had already said he was not going to compromise the message and now he was saying he has recorded a song that has no message at all. It's just a rock and roll number. The same story quoted him as saying he "quit rock and roll to follow Jesus."

What gives?

In a meeting with Mylon and a number of others in August 1986, he was asked, "Why did you record a secular album?" His answer:

> I'm going to get it out on Top 40 radio stations. When I
> go to town, I'm going to bill it as a rock and roll show. Get
> kids to come to a rock concert. Then I'm going to preach to
> them about Jesus.

This is not the way the Gospel works. You don't become a prostitute to win prostitutes — that's prostitution. Is that what religious rock has become? *A form of prostitution?* As remote as that possibility might seem — if temple prostitutes could justify themselves, so could a host of others.

Rez Band

Rez Band, originally called Resurrection Band, emerged from the Jesus movement of the late 1960s and early 1970s. Just like many others in the religious realm, Rez is another of those bands now approaching the secular rock audience.

According to a published story (*CCM*/April 1986):

> . . . Rez Band expects to keep their musical orientation essentially the same as it's always been — raw, muscular rock 'n' roll accented by the Kaisers' no-nonsense vocals and by Heiss' blistering guitar.
>
> "On our previous album, *Hostage*," remarks Herrin, "we were enticed into the realm of more keyboards and drum machines — which seemed like nice little toys to play with. But I don't think we, as a whole, felt that comfortable with them.
>
> "On *Between Heaven 'N' Hell*, we were able to bring ourselves back to our roots. We are more of a guitar/live drum rock 'n' roll band, and I think we're gonna stay that way. We hope to stay a little rawer than what's going on in the area of slick production."

It's in the area of production that Rez is considering some extensive changes like many others, according to the article:

> The up-to-now self-produced band has been talking to engineer Ron St. Germain, whose knob-twisting credits include the Rolling Stones, Mick Jagger's solo project, and the Duran Duran spinoff, Arcadia.

That kind of change fits neatly into the secular image the band apparently is courting. A girl who attended one of the group's first bookings by its new agency wrote the following letter to a magazine:

> I had the privilege of attending one of their first
> concerts booked by their new agency at a nightclub in
> Milwaukee. I was very proud to be a Christian that night.

I can't imagine any reason for feeling pride with such a
group playing in a nightclub. It seems weeping would be
the more correct emotion.

Rez has consistently drawn hot reaction from people
who have been exposed to either its music or theology. The
band, part of an organization known as Jesus People USA,
publishes a magazine, *Cornerstone*, in which the following letter appeared in Volume 15, Issue 79:

> . . . Your statement, "We're all, everyone, unrighteous
> sinners" does nothing to glorify God — an attitude and
> result I see is quite common amongst "Christian rockers."
> Christian hearts are not "desperate and deceitfully
> wicked" as you say, but God has written His law there;
> indeed, God has given us new hearts (Ezekiel 36:26)!
> False humility is no substitute for holiness. Neither is the
> compromise and corruption of "Christian rock" a profit-
> able substitute for us to be a peculiar people who show
> forth praises of our God — not comformed to this world
> with punk rock hairdos, garb, and music, but transformed
> by the renewing of our minds.
>
> So your vision is to live out Matthew 25:40 "As you
> did it unto one of the least of these My brethren, you did it
> unto Me."
>
> Consider then what you're doing to thousands of
> impressionable Christian youth: exhorting them to punk
> out, rock on, and to consider as "common" that which the
> Lord Jesus Christ has made clear (namely our hearts).
> Instead of leading youth to be holy, righteous, and bold to
> make a stand against this wicked and perverse generation,
> you're making them to be twofold more the child of hell
> than yourselves. . . .

Petra

Perhaps more so than any other group in religious rock,
the group Petra — after some fifteen years and nine albums

— has demonstrated the growth and appeal of this music medium, which has now created a new industry.

Begun in 1972 by four Bible college students in Fort Wayne, Indiana, the group soon began playing its "primitive," high-decibel music at schools, colleges, parks, and prisons, as well as the Adam's Apple, a local Christian center. Its first album was released in 1974 as a kind of "test balloon" for religious rock. Another harder-edged release followed three years later.

Today when Petra hits the road, an army of equipment follows:

• Three 52-foot semi-trucks, with an additional 24-foot truck and two buses,

• Thirty-two sound cabinets carrying more than 15,000 watts of power,

• Four hundred lights with 400,000 watts of power, all run by a computerized control board,

• Ten tons of stage gear for suspending the lights and sound equipment in mid-air,

• A twenty-member crew of technicians and drivers.

That, in a nutshell, tells you something of the growth of religious rock — a group which began as four Bible college students now tours Australia, Norway, Canada, and amusement parks in the U.S. and sells some 300,000 copies of each album. The band, which recorded their version of "God Gave Rock and Roll to You" on two different albums, is faithful to its rock music roots in its musical approach. According to an article in the October 1986 issue of *Contemporary Christian Magazine*:

> *Back to the Street*, with its bigger, punchier rock delivery, rivals the AOR sound of giants like Journey, Kansas, and Boston . . .
>
> The real focus for the band on *Back to the Street* was to create a fresh, rock 'n' roll identity. . . .

The article noted that Petra's new album produced several firsts: "a new vocalist, two new producers, and a revitalized rock sound. . . ." The project is the first Christian album for its two producers.

> [John] Schlitt is quick to give credit around the board for the band's *rockier* bent. "The *harsher type sound* of my voice did dictate a change for Petra," he admits, "but when I joined the group we all agreed that this was the direction we wanted to go anyway." (Italics mine.)

Like many other religious rock groups, Petra's sound appears to be getting heavier and harder. Yet, unlike others, Petra seems to know the world is not listening to its music; the church is.

Founder Bob Hartman says, "Many of the songs are directed to the body of Christ. That, after all, is our audience."

> Hartman is realistic about who hears Petra's message. "There are not going to be a lot of non-Christians just walking in and spending their money to see a Christian band."

In spite of the fact that Petra's audience is the church, look at the influence and intent of the group's music:

> Schlitt: ". . . I'm really active on stage. I think that comes from my experiences in *secular rock*." (Italics mine.)
>
> Hartman: "It'll be more aggressive. People will notice that right away. We are intending to come out more than ever before as a rock band."

Amy Grant

Of course, no listing of the superstars of religious rock would be complete without the name of Amy Grant, who has sold more records — four million at last count — than anyone else in the so-called contemporary realm.

In a *Charisma* magazine interview, July 1986, Ms. Grant was asked the following question:

"You are a role model. What do you want other Christian women to emulate in you?"

Her reply:

> Uh-oh. That's scary. I guess I don't look at myself like that, like a role model, in that people will emulate what I do. . . .

It is almost inconceivable that this young woman doesn't see herself as a role model, or that she doesn't grasp the influence of the role she portrays to others. The book *What About Christian Rock?* notes:

> Of course, young people who enjoy Christian music may mimic the life-styles of their favorite artists too. Once again, fashions are the most obvious, but some young fans also walk like, talk like, and look like their Christian music heroes. When Amy Grant bounces onstage in her baggy, leopard-print jacket, dozens of Grant groupies in the audience display similarly spotted attire. . . .

In that same *Charisma* interview, the young lady from Nashville responded to a question about her so-called crossover:

> . . . I want to communicate with my peers. By getting into pop music, I am saying I want to be a voice in my culture. I'm not always thrilled about what my culture is saying. So I throw myself into this arena that sometimes is distasteful to me also. . . .

What about Christian Rock? offered her some advice in that regard:

It is also true, however, that if Grant [or any artist] is grooming to be a major crossover entertainer — appealing to the non-Christian as well as the Christian — she must develop the wisdom and finesse necessary to deal with a demanding media. She must overcome childish impetuousness, and strive toward thoughtful consideration of every remark, every action.

I wonder if Ms. Grant thought about being a voice in her culture or what impact would be made on those she influences by her latest recording (at this writing) of a love song, "The Next Time I Fall," a duet with rock singer Peter Cetera, formerly of the group Chicago.

The song, complete with a music video featuring Grant/Cetera as young lovers and skimpily dressed dancers in sensual movements in the background, landed in the Top 10 for a brief time. The pair also reportedly appeared to sing the song on TV's "Solid Gold," arguably one of the most licentious programs on the air, bordering on pornographic, with its lurid dancers.

Ms. Grant also performed with Ricky Skaggs on the 1986 Country Music Association's Awards Show. The duo did "Walkin' in Jerusalem," an old spiritual on Skaggs' new album.

Evidently, that kind of appearance doesn't bother Ms. Grant. After all, that's show biz.

It has been suggested that what Ms. Grant does would fall under the category of "sanctified entertainment. It has all the diversionary value of entertainment, but it is infused with the power of the gospel."

These words all sound so noble, so intellectually bright, so precisely considered.

Yet, the hard-edged honest truth is that Amy Grant's public statements, stage performances, and general musical direction seem woeful for someone who is supposed to be a role model for millions of young people.

CHAPTER
TEN

RELIGIOUS ROCK AND THE CHURCH

e don't seem to have a word for "wrong" anymore in the moral sense, as in "theft is wrong."
— Meg Greenfield in *Newsweek*

Religious rock music could have never reached the place of such broad and open acceptance today without a number of divergent forces in the church world working in concert to influence that reception.

To better understand the response religious rock has received, one must examine the facets in the church world — religious TV networks, magazines, and influential churches — which have aided this musical genre.

Rock Music Videos

All three religious television networks — CBN, PTL, TBN — as well as several individual gospel TV stations, have contributed to the music's popularity by spotlighting artists and groups which utilize the rock sound.

CBN's "700 Club" has a special entertainment reporter who highlights stories of Christians working in show business, while both PTL and TBN's flagship interview programs frequently use artists who play religious rock.

In fact, Stryper's inside cover for its latest release, *To Hell with the Devil,* extends thanks to a number of individuals and companies for their help, including Pat Boone and Jim and Tammy Bakker.

The 16-year-old daughter of the Bakkers, Tammy Sue, has recently released her first album, *Sixteen,* which she described as, "It's reggae and it's rock 'n' roll."

With the widespread popularity of the Music Television Video (MTV) Network highlighting popular secular rock groups, an identical effort has been underway for several years to popularize videos from religious rock.

All of religious rock's superstars — Amy Grant, Mylon LeFevre, Leon Patillo, Petra, DeGarmo and Key, Stryper, Steve Taylor, Rez Band, Randy Stonehill — and a host of lesser lights have all put together music videos.

DeGarmo and Key's video production of "Six, Six, Six" was temporarily turned down by MTV because of a human figure in flames. The revised product — showing a man representing the antichrist gazing into a crystal ball — was duly programmed by MTV on light rotation.

Typical of the videos is Mylon LeFevre's "Stranger to Danger," which portrays the Holy Spirit as riding on a motorcycle seeking out Mylon, who is supposed to be a lost, tormented soul. In the end, Mylon heeds the call and invites others to follow. The video closes with him and his band singing, "I'm gonna be like Jesus."

For several years, PTL has had a program called "Sound Effects" which is aired twice a day on Saturday.

TBN has a similar program hosted by the son of the network's founder.

Not to be left behind, the Christian Broadcasting Network (CBN) began production of "Fast Forward" on a weekly basis beginning January 3, 1987.

According to producer Norman Mintle, "Fast Forward is targeted to reach 14 to 24-year-old Christian young people. We're projecting the show to reach into at least one million households per week."

Rock Christian Network (RCN), a new satellite television outreach sponsored by Rock Church, Virginia Beach, Virginia, is producing a music video program of its own, as well as utilizing the "Off the Wall" show produced by Airborn Communications.

However, the use of these artists, either as talk show guests or by promoting this genre of music through a video, gives added legitimacy to religious rock.

In fact, if someone has a question about the music's authenticity, that question will be resolved in the minds of some people when they see the rock medium embraced by respected Christian leaders. That's like an outright endorsement.

If there is any doubt in anyone's mind, that will be quickly dispelled when a particular TV network provides an outlet for religious rock.

Publications

Several publications are currently being published which address themselves specifically to the religious rock music scene. *Christian Activities Calendar, Harvest Rock Syndicate,* and *Cornerstone* are fairly typical of those publications. However, all three have limited circulation.

In fact, *Harvest Rock Syndicate,* apparently in its first year or so of operation, received the following letter from the manager of a Christian bookstore connected to Billy Graham's ministry in Minneapolis:

> I am not able to carry your paper at this time, nor would I be interested in carrying it in the future. This is not a periodical that my customers would accept. I hope you do not take this as a put down. I personally was very impressed with the caliber of reporting in your publication, but I have rules and standards I must uphold when considering items to be put in the bookstore. . . .

The Saturday Evening Post has carried polite cover stories on religious rock artists such as Amy Grant, as has *Charisma*, which has a circulation of nearly 150,000 among mostly Charismatic and Pentecostal subscribers. *Charisma*'s Amy Grant story promised "A Candid Interview That Goes Beyond the Controversy." Yet the article in the July 1986 issue was incredibly tame.

February 1987's edition of *Charisma* featured a cover story on pop singer Denise Williams, a Christian, who also records gospel music. The issue also included an excerpt from *What About Gospel Rock?* and information on the magazine's 1987 Music Poll.

Since *Charisma* runs frequent advertisements from record companies, perhaps that could best explain the magazine's tender treatment of religious rock.

In fact, *Ministries Today,* a sister publication to *Charisma*, recently carried a cover story on Religious Rock in the church with an interview featuring Mylon LeFevre and his pastor, Dr. Paul Walker, as examples.

The boldest step *Charisma* has taken with the religious rockers came in its December 1986 issue when it recommended "a Christmas shopping list which you can draw from when looking for a gift album."

Among those albums listed was:

> *Solitude/Solitaire* by Peter Cetera includes a dazzling duet with Amy Grant. "The Next Time I Fall" has already climbed into the *Billboard* magazine Top 20 and still has momentum. It's the kind of love song that brought applause and criticism with "Find a Way."

To label that secular duet "dazzling" and recommend its purchase to Christians is absolutely beneath the dignity of *Charisma*'s motto: "The Magazine About Spirit-led Living."

Yet it is exactly this kind of effort which is being expended in the Body of Christ to bring religious rock into respectability. *Charisma*'s influence among its readers aids that cause.

CHRISTIAN CONTEMPORARY MAGAZINE

Although its circulation is relatively minor (actually less than 40,000) when compared to a publication like *Charisma, Christian Contemporary Magazine*, now known as *CCM*, still has a considerable influence among its readers, radio stations, and bookstores.

If there is a publication anywhere that is pro-religious rock, it is *CCM*.

Not only is *CCM* enthusiastic in its endorsement of religious rock — no matter the variety or weirdness of the genre — but it has taken a number of verbal slaps at myself, David Wilkerson, and anybody else who raises a voice against religious rock.

The October 1986 edition is a prime example. Under the magazine's Insider column appeared the following:

> HOW LONG, O LORD? — If you haven't heard by now, evangelist Jimmy Swaggart is on the rampage again. This time, his tirade is against the over 900 Wal-Mart and K-Mart stores to discontinue stocking a number of rock

> albums and rock-oriented magazines. Problem is, it
> basically worked. The chain has indeed pulled a selection
> of album titles off the racks along with 35 magazines,
> including the well-known purveyor of satanic slime, *Tiger
> Beat.* . . .

By *CCM*'s comments, it seems the publication is placing its seal of approval on all rock magazines directed at teenagers. How could anyone advocate the filth which passes for reading material being acceptable for this nation's young people?

Of course, the magazine that I mentioned over television which brought the response from Wal-Mart came from *Hit Parader,* not *Tiger Beat.*

However, my great concern is the apparent endorsement which *CCM* — supposedly operated by Christians — unwittingly gave to the rock magazine industry, to say nothing of the condescending attitude toward Jimmy Swaggart in its article.

In a letter to my son, Donnie, *CCM* Publisher John Styll wrote, "Several of our readers have expressed a similar concern about the column."

One woman wrote *CCM* to say:

> Although I disagree with him [Jimmy Swaggart]
> greatly and think he is narrow-minded about Christian
> rock, I agree with what he is doing this time. What is the
> problem with him getting a selection of album titles and
> 35 magazines, including Tiger Beat, off the rack? I've
> never seen anything in Tiger Beat that glorifies the Lord. I
> think what he's doing is great. . . .

Of course, *CCM*'s answer centered around the issue of censorship, a cry that is often heard by people in the media.

Styll's letter to Donnie stated in part, "We hope that young people will find in it [*CCM*] a *healthy, upbuilding alternative* to the trash that is being offered to them at every turn." (Italics mine.)

Yet the magazine's November 1986 issue quoted a base, vulgar obscenity from singer Steve Camp.

Letters to *CCM*, in its January 1987 issue, strongly questioned that obscenity being used:

> . . . Near the end of your terrific article, why did you have to ruin the whole thing by printing the profane language? Was that the only way Steve could vent his anger at other entertainers' lack of responsibility toward giving their fans the gospel? . . .
>
> Unfortunately . . . as I was soaking up all these intellectual gems, I came across . . . THE WORD. Now here is where my argument comes in: Everyone who read the article knows exactly what word I am referring to, and I believe that many were just as offended as this "sorry excuse for an open-minded college student" was . . . I'm just a stupid kid who hasn't learned that words are just *words* and that vulgarity only appears when words are put in a sequence where there is malicious or harmful intent. Okay, okay, but *you* explain that to the high school guys I'm discipling. . . .

Another writer in that same issue canceled his subscription citing:

> . . . The caricature of Mr. Swaggart, ads for metal "Christian" rock that have various demonic covers, your extremely unchristian attitude in various articles in the issue . . . I will no longer receive your magazine, and it sickens me to think that people like you are using the Lord for profit and giving the rest of the world a bad example of Christianity. I am a journalist and pray that I can use my talents for the Lord in a much better way than you people who have massacred any good intentions in your effort.

Churches

Three churches — Mount Paran Church of God in Atlanta, Georgia, Warehouse Ministries in Sacramento, California, and the Carpenter's Home Church in Lakeland, Florida — are characteristic of those local churches which utilize religious rock as a part of their outreach programs.

The Carpenter's Home Church was formerly known as the First Assembly of God before its move to a new location near Lake Gibson and the construction of a 10,000-seat auditorium. In the past year, the church has sponsored concerts with religious rocker Leon Patillo, Carman, and Kim Boyce.

A Sunday night program at the church in connection with evangelist Rex Humbard featured country music's Ricky Skaggs, a Christian, who sang three gospel songs. The night prior, Skaggs had appeared at the Lakeland Civic Center with both Willie Nelson and Hank Williams, Jr.

Carpenter's Home Church operates a 100,000-watt radio station, WCIE, 24 hours a day, under a commercial-free, educational grant license.

Like some 1,600 religious radio stations in the country, WCIE plays a variety of musical styles, besides broadcasting the Carpenter's Home Church services as well as several other church-related programs.

However, the station's predominate sound is religious rock. The use of religious rock over the air has evidently created a market for the records, tapes, and videos of the artists. The church's bookstore, located off the main lobby, has an extensive collection of materials on the religious rockers including Amy Grant, Michael W. Smith, Rez Band, Stryper, Bash-N-The Code, and a host of others.

Posters in the bookstore and announcements over the station (in late December 1986) announced the appearance of religious rocker Rick Cua "in concert" in the area. The radio station, which has its own monthly newsletter and prints a Top 40 list of popular songs, sounds much like a secular counterpart at certain times of the day with the harder-edged sound.

Church Pastor Karl Strader said at a recent "Idea Exchange" meeting, "I don't even like contemporary music . . . I don't even listen to our own radio station."

Warehouse Ministries

Warehouse Ministries, a church located in an industrial park off I-50 in Sacramento, is known for its use of religious rock in regularly held concerts. The congregation, pastored by Louis Neely, holds three Sunday morning services for its church of some 1,500.

The pastor's wife, Mary, founded Exit Records in 1982 and has since recorded several who attend the church including Charlie Peacock and members of Vector and the 77s. Ms. Neely is also the co-author of the book, *Stairway to Heaven*.

CCM gave Ms. Neely credit "for building virtually from scratch much of the organized new music culture in Sacramento."

Evidently much of that culture is based in secular rock and roll and playing in bars. At least that's the impression *CCM* gives in its May 1986 issue: "Although bigger clubs like Harry's Bar, The Watchtower, and The Club Can't Tell (downtown's venerable old jazz refuge) host many of the bands from time to time."

While in Sacramento for a Stryper concert (that was canceled), this book's co-author called Warehouse Ministries to inquire if any of the church's groups would be playing anywhere locally.

"I believe Charlie Peacock will be at Melarkey's downtown," the secretary suggested.

In calling Melarkey's number in the telephone directory, he was told the business was a restaurant *and bar.* Evidently that's where some of Sacramento's religious rockers play.

The church has recently held concerts with Rez Band, Charlie Peacock, and Bloodgood. It was reported that young people have committed their lives to Christ from the concerts. However, since no concerts were being held while this book's co-author was in town, this cannot be verified.

What I can verify is that religious rock artists from the church do play in local bars. The music, which has been described as "a punchy brand of eclectic pop/jazz rock" apparently appeals to that clientele.

Mount Paran Church of God

Since Mylon LeFevre has gained considerable attention through his religious rock songs, his home church, Mount Paran Church of God in Atlanta, has also received exposure due to its use of the rock music in its youth programs.

The church has, in fact, employed four religious rock bands for use at its Monday night youth meetings for the church of some 8,000, pastored by Dr. Paul Walker.

Having read about Mount Paran's efforts in using religious rock, this book's co-author attended two Monday night meetings at Mount Paran. The first Monday night in January, the group "Alternative" — a five-man rock band — performed for the benefit of less than 100 young people.

Between piercing guitar riffs, crushing drums, and flashing red/blue/yellow lights, Alternative played and periodically read Scriptures between songs. People wandered in and out of the building continually. An unshaven Mylon LeFevre even dropped by to check out the schedule.

The crowd — if it could be called that — seemed bored with everything happening that night.

Two weeks later, David Teems and The Calling (a church band) appeared with nationally known Morgan Cryer and his band. A crowd of some 300 were on hand representing four Baptist churches, two Church of God congregations, and one Assemblies of God. Church buses and vans in the parking lot attested to their attendance.

David Teems closed his performance playing a blue electric fiddle in a "hoedown" fashion while the audience clapped, danced, and patted their feet.

Morgan Cryer's four mop-top musicians practically blew the walls of the building down with the loudness of their instruments. His band, dressed in punk fashions of leather and slouchy clothes, danced and rocked for about 45 minutes. Cryer shared his testimony of growing up as a "nerd" between songs.

Throughout the concert, the young people clapped, danced, and stomped their feet to the music. After some 45 minutes, Cryer closed with his song, "Pray in the U.S.A.", and gave an altar call.

Nobody budged.

After an extended wait, the call was changed to those "who need a closer walk." Perhaps five or ten people responded to that . . . and the concert ended.

For all of the hype and fancy words about evangelistic programs using religious rock, the audience turned out to be simply church kids. The idea of employing religious rock to reach them seemed totally out of place. It was certainly unnecessary for the results achieved.

CHAPTER
ELEVEN

WHAT'S AHEAD?

hile sister Christian groups, Undercover and The Altar Boys, flirt with a more accessible sound, O.B.P. is just plain raw. A Christian Banned belongs next to The Dead Kennedys or an unmentionable mainstream group whose members included Johnny Rotten and Sid Vicious.

— One Bad Pig's album review in *Harvest Rock Syndicate*

In the last year, the foremost trend among the religious rockers has become obvious. These performers are going to become more easily identified with the world.

From my research, as well as concerts attended by my staff, there is no question that the music is taking a rawer, louder approach with most groups — while some are steering their direction totally secular although they desperately want the support of the Christian community.

Last year when several of the religious rockers and others involved in gospel music met in Baton Rouge to talk with me, one of the preachers present made a statement I've never forgotten.

"Very shortly," he said, "the heaviest rock will be the norm in all of our churches."

Now this preacher is not a youngster just starting in the ministry. He is a man in his early 70s, with the highest degrees our universities and seminaries can bestow. He has served as president of Bible colleges and is considered to be a noted Bible authority.

Although I would strongly disagree that the music will ever become the norm in church, the heavy rock sound clearly seems characteristic of what the industry wants and what the musicians are willing to appeasingly give their record producers.

Secular companies for the last several years have observed this trend developing with religious rock and they are going to step in for their piece of the pie and record these artists. Of course, their interest is purely monetary — nothing more and nothing less.

I predict that the record companies will stay with the religious rock trend as long as the money continues to flow or until another trend develops and everybody jumps on that particular musical wave.

The whole spectrum of religious rock — heavy metal, Top 40, punk, new wave, jazz/rock, even the trash metal — will continue to head in the identical direction until people won't be able to tell the difference between a religious rock song and a secular one. That's virtually the case already.

Gut Level Music

Contemporary Christian Magazine (June 1986 issue) profiled a new group, The Altar Boys, in the following manner:

> Their simple but honest raw music, often confused
> with punk, is both fun and frantic, refreshing and *annoying*
> . . . . (Italics mine.)

According to the trio, their album, *When You're a Rebel,* was for Christians "but there was some evangelistic stuff mixed in. Our next album will be specifically for non-Christians, saying things they can understand. A more gut-level thing."

The record, *Gut Level Music,* has already been released.

The group is quoted as saying:

> . . . We have to get it into the major record stores . . .
> To be able to pick it up in a normal record store gives it
> credibility with a larger audience — which is what we
> want. . . .

Do you recognize the quest for credibility with most of these new groups? Credibility to them is having a record in a "normal record store."

> *"There is no fear of God before their eyes"*
> (Rom. 3:18).

The article continues, quoting the group's guitarist/singer Mike Stand: "And I feel God has called us to reach both sides. It's just that most Christian albums are for both, and we felt we should do one that speaks directly and totally to the non-Christians."

What follows is a series of confusing, contradictory sentences in the article — but, then again, that seems typical of the religious rockers:

> Don't think the band plans to hide their candle under a
> bushel, though. At least one song is blatant: "I'm Not

Talking About Religion," which goes on to "not talk about" just a belief, just going to church, *just shaving your head. The lyrics clearly point to a relationship with God.* (Italics mine.)

Do you get the solid impression that the world's influence has taken over the lyrics, the style, and the musical approach of these musicians? And yet this is all supposed to represent God? Nothing could be further from the truth. Why don't we try to redeem the culture instead of imitate it?

> *"For the time will come when they will not endure sound doctrine; but after their own lusts shall they heap to themselves teachers, having itching ears;*
> *"And they shall turn away their ears from the truth, and shall be turned unto fables"* (II Tim. 4:3, 4).

Bourgeois Tagg, Vector, the 77s

According to a *Contemporary Christian Magazine article* (May 1986), the city of Sacramento — California's capital — has become the birthplace of a number of new groups such as Bourgeois Tagg, Vector, the 77s, and Charlie Peacock.

Listen to some of the comments from the story:

> Bourgeois Tagg, formed three years ago . . . is leading the Sacramento pack down the road to the big time. Their slick "mod-pop" sound, walking the balance between Duran Duran and Mr. Mister, captured the watchful eye of Britain's Island Records.
>
> Looking to make its presence more known stateside, the label sports other signees such as U2 and Frankie Goes to Hollywood.

What the story's author doesn't tell you about the group known as "Frankie Goes to Hollywood" is that it has recorded one of the filthiest pornographic albums ever made. That's the company the new religious rock groups are keeping.

> *"Their throat is an open sepulchre; with their tongues they have used deceit; the poison of asps is under their lips:*
> *"Whose mouth is full of cursing and bitterness: Their feet are swift to shed blood:*
> *"Destruction and misery are in their ways"*
> (Rom. 3:13-16).

Jim Abegg, lead guitarist for the group named "Vector," made the following statement in the *CCM* story:

> There are some good clubs in Sacramento, but there really isn't a big enough population base here to make a decent and consistent living. Anybody can go out and play to two or three hundred people every weekend, but it doesn't get you anywhere.

Do you sense the calling of God in that statement or do you possibly feel that individual is just into the music scene for the financial benefits? Basically, the group's background, as well as several others mentioned in the article, appears to be the club circuit.

Vector's Steve Griffith characterized the band in the following manner:

> We have a diverse lineup. And right now I think that we're putting together credible material. Jim and I have been playing together for a few years. And Bruce Spencer, our drummer, just turned 20, so he's into a lot of current

influences — Prince, Phil Collins, etc. That gives us an interesting balance.

Do you catch the phrase *influence*?

That's the key word as to where the new religious rock bands get their inspiration — the music of the world. In the case of the singer known as Prince, his music and stage performances all suggest sexually deviate behavior.

The religious rockers' approach all seem to suggest: "We must become the world to win the world." That method will not work — period!

Another Sacramento group, the 77s, is called the "we-play-what-we-please rockers." Co-founder and bassist, Jan Eric Volz, was quoted as saying:

> We do the music we like. Over the years we've welded elements of everyone from Elvis to the Smiths. We stick to our guns from playing only basic rock 'n' roll — American music.

The same kind of spirit in Volz's comment was echoed by The Altar Boys' Stand when asked about the band's music future:

> More raw. Just pound. And just gutsier. We're going to strip our sound down to the core and bang away because that's what the kids are responding to. We don't care what critics say. We just feel called to play stripped-down rock 'n' roll. No eyeshadow. Just an honest, unpolished band. . . .

That's typical for most of the religious rockers. Yet as trends come and go, the world's influence can make some of the groups seem very tame compared to newer arrivals on the scene. The Austin, Texas, based group known as "One Bad Pig" is a case in point.

One Bad Pig

According to an article (Volume 15, Issue 79) in *Cornerstone* magazine, the idea for One Bad Pig started out as a joke for a local religious rock festival . . . yet "the response was so favorable, and we realized the stuff was really powerful and could be more than just a joke."

The publication described the band's performance at a music festival:

> A conservative-looking young man walked across the stage and into the spotlight. "Is everybody ready to pig out?" he shouted. Yeeah! "Then let's have a warm *Cornerstone* welcome for ONE BAD PIG!" The metal barn shook on its cold cement slab as three pale, skinny guys slunk onto the stage. They looked the part — if the part called for abject terror — and they hid from the unforgiving spotlight behind guitar, bass, and drums. THIS IS SO STINKING GREAT! and the joke was still in the telling when two hundred fifty pounds of punchline strutted onto center stage. He brandished aloft, like Hulk Hogan waving a vanquished Woody Allen, an electric guitar, which exploded in an unexpected white-hot flash, and its master beat it senseless against the hollow wooden stage. "Don't slam your brothers and sisters, slam the devil." Between frenetic, noisy songs, "lead screamer" Kosher tried to calm the crowd from frenzy mindless to mindful . . .
>
> The crowd thinned out as the joke wore off for some, now exhausted from laughing at polka-punk songs like "Loony Tune." Others who found the joke not the least little bit funny had mass exited before the end of the first song ("This IS NOT of God!"). You couldn't blame anyone for cruising out into the cool night air. The music was terrible, the sound was worse, the air was unbearable. But for the people who stayed, the experience was authentic and the event was wholly up to the hype. . . .

The magazine described the group's leader as saying:

> It's Jesus in your face — that's what One Bad Pig is
> really. Our lyrics are blunt and simple — I'm no poet —
> and that fits the punk medium: repetitive, to the point.
> Take it or leave it. . . .

There's not one question in my mind: *I'll leave it.* The
fact that a group such as this could even be invited to
perform at a so-called religious music festival shows the
absolute degeneracy of the entire medium.

Yet One Bad Pig has already recorded its first album, *A
Christian Banned*, on the Porky's Demise label. Even one
religious rock publication wrote, "The real issue behind a
Christian punk LP isn't whether or not O.B.P. has anything
to say, but rather, is anyone still listening?"

What's Ahead?

This is typical of what's ahead for religious rock. New
groups — all with some sort of trendy musical gimmick —
are characteristic of the medium.

This book could have been literally filled with the
names of new groups and their message — Adam Again,
4°4°1, Barren Cross, D.O.X., Philadelphia, Messiah
Prophet, Omega Sunrise, Wild Blue Yonder, Allies. Yet
before the ink would have dried on the pages, a host of new
bands would have arrived on the scene.

That's the nature of the music industry which follows
one trend right after another.

What deeply saddens and troubles my heart is the fact
the music is becoming harder, rawer, more worldly — if
that's possible — all the time. The religious rock music is
flawed at its foundation. It has no basis in Scripture, and
that flaw becomes more obvious every day with the arrival
of a new band — cruder, louder, and more suggestive than
the last group.

The flaw can't correct itself. It will only widen.

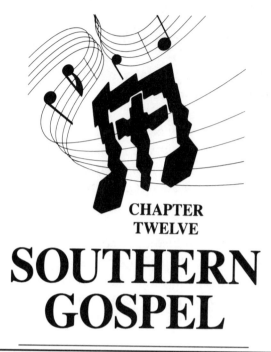

CHAPTER TWELVE

SOUTHERN GOSPEL

A *nd on Sundays and Wednesdays — Wednesdays being revival days at the First Assembly of God Church — Elvis learned to sing spirituals.*
— from *Elvis* by Jerry Hopkins

Since the Rev. Thomas A. Dorsey, known as "the father of gospel," wrote "Precious Lord, Take My Hand" in 1932, gospel music has been a popular form of musical expression, particularly in the south where it seems to have become a part of the fabric of the land.

During the 1940s and 1950s, the southern gospel quartet trend began with groups like the Statesmen Quartet, the Blackwood Brothers, and others, establishing a pattern which still exists today. The groups were virtual carbon copies — complete with four-part harmony, matching suits, and crowd-pleasing stage antics.

Of course, the music has ventured through trends over the years with trios and mixed groups with female voices. Also, the instrumentation has experienced pronounced change beyond a simple piano to include three and sometimes four other instruments.

Southern gospel as an industry has been riddled with problems from the very beginning. The star syndrome and competition between groups are just as prevalent as they are in religious rock. Most of the quartet convention-style programs are hardly anything beyond a "show," seldom leading anyone to either salvation or a deeper walk with Christ.

The industry has also been considerably corrupted by immorality among its participants, and alcoholism. This book's co-author wrote the revealing account ten years ago of the late James Sego, of "Sego Brothers and Naomi," who had been an alcoholic for many years while active in gospel music.

Several groups have also left the southern gospel field for secular music. The Oak Ridge Boys, once known as the Oak Ridge Quartet, is probably the best known — now singing what is often a raunchy form of country music.

The Dixie Melody Boys, a group that began in southern gospel, recently changed its name to the DMB Band after several years of changing musical direction. The band's music is "a progressive country sound." *Christian Activities Calendar* calls the sound a unique blend of contemporary Christian/country music.

Does It Edify?

Churches which employ southern gospel groups oftentimes are encouraging the unholy mixture of the world and God. That's because most of these so-called gospel concerts are nothing more than a "show" where performers are entertaining.

The issue has nothing to do with a person's musical taste, or likes and dislikes for particular music. I'm speaking of what is right and wrong spiritually, what is biblical, what is Christ-glorifying, and what is Christlike.

The Apostle Paul looked at it in this manner:

> *"All things are lawful for me, but all things*
> *are not expedient: all things are lawful for me,*
> *but all things edify not"* (I Cor. 10:23).

Paul is speaking about edification of the Body of Christ and Christ Himself. A person can involve himself in many things which may not be sinful on the surface but which do not edify Christ. Thus, there is no spiritual profit.

Several years ago I appeared on the "700 Club" and this subject was addressed. The program's co-host asked, "Are you telling me Bing Crosby's 'White Christmas' is wrong?"

My answer was this:

> It's not a question of being right or wrong. It's a
> question of being edifying. The truth is, it's not edifying to
> the cause of Christ. It does not glorify or lift up Jesus
> Christ.

A Christian really doesn't have to look at some situation and ask whether it's sinful or not. The proper question is, rather: Does it edify Christ? Does it glorify Christ? The sin question is answered easily once the edification question is addressed.

I strongly believe that much of the southern gospel quartet music falls into this category.

An Interview

Janet Paschal, one of our featured soloists, probably sings to more people today than any other female singer.

Yet before she joined this Ministry, Janet traveled the southern gospel music circuit for almost seven years. The following interview with Robert Paul Lamb reflects her experiences and impressions from those years "on the circuit."

R.P. — *How did you get started in singing gospel music?*

Janet — I was raised in the church and first began singing there. At eighteen, I auditioned for a gospel group and was hired.

R.P. — *What was the situation you found in gospel music once you began traveling the circuit?*

Janet — When I first joined the group, they were sort of at a low point due to personnel changes. As a result, we appeared in a lot of churches, as opposed to concerts in auditoriums. Of course, that gradually changed over the years.

I suppose I grew up thinking all these singers were anointed of the Lord. That's not to say some aren't. But I was thinking they were more so than what I discovered when I got into the circuit. Perhaps at eighteen, I had stars in my eyes. I also found there was a lot of hard work involved. I probably went through a period of being disillusioned.

R.P. — *What happened to effect this feeling of being disillusioned?*

Janet — Well, a lot of our concerts included four or five major groups. People talked about wanting to leave the stage "hot" from a rousing song. You might have groups not wanting to follow other particular groups on stage. There might be an argument over how much time one group got while another took less. Everything was more business oriented than I'd ever guessed.

I just thought everybody got up there with the program they felt the Lord had given them and sang. I felt it shouldn't matter where they came in the program.

R.P. — *Would you say the programs were more performance-oriented as opposed to being ministry?*

Janet — They were more performance-oriented. Of course, there were exceptions. But the programs were pretty much planned out — the introductions, the funny lines, the order of songs. A program was basically followed for a year, then changed.

R.P. — *What about preparation? Was there prayer before going on stage? Did the group ever have Bible study together?*

Janet — No, not as far as I knew. Again, there may have been exceptions but I'm saying as far as I knew. Inner preparation didn't seem to have anything to do with it, or you could say, it was left totally up to the individual.

When I joined the group, I made up my mind that I would read something from the Bible every day, no matter the schedule. Of course, we were traveling frequently and doing one-night stands. We'd go to bed on the bus one night and wake up the next morning in the town where we would be in the next concert. But I continued reading my Bible every night and just spending time with the Lord.

Because of that, I believe the Lord helped me see things as they were as opposed to becoming a part of them. This helped set me apart and enabled me to say, "That's not the way I want to be."

R.P. — *In gospel music circles, are people there because of the calling of God or just a host of other reasons?*

Janet — Let me say that I personally worked with a good group of people who were very sincere. But as far as the calling of God is concerned, I think most of the people in the gospel quartet circuit are there for other reasons. Their family might have been in the business; that's very prevalent. It was just rare to see somebody who was there because it was God's calling on their life.

R.P. — *In terms of results, were people saved in the churches where you sang? Were altar calls given?*

Janet — It did happen where individuals said they gave their heart to the Lord during the service or at some place where a particular song was sung. But it was rare. Some pastors might have given altar calls, in which case people would have responded.

R.P. — *I suppose it could be said that you found that persons and personalities were glorified in gospel music and that the financial aspect of the business overshadowed much of what was done?*

Janet — Yes, but I think that is something that has evolved in gospel music. I don't think it started that way. The people who started were sincere, and of course there are still some sincere people there. But I believe the growth of gospel music and the business aspect of selling records have affected this.

R.P. — *Would you say this affects the industry with current trends today?*

Janet — Sure. You can detect that with the contemporary fad. Gospel music kind of goes along with whatever is going. It began with quartets, shifted over to trios, then more towards female voices. Now it's moving in a contemporary vein. Yet it doesn't change according to the message God has given. It moves only with the trends.

When I was traveling with the group, we were with a major record label. So we had to pick songs our producers liked. Songs that would "chart." That would cause the records to be played regularly over the radio, giving us visibility and familiarity with listeners and promoters.

R.P — *After all that time traveling, what would you say was your biggest disappointment?*

Janet — I guess a lack of total dedication from people to the Lord Himself. A lot of times groups on the road would stay in the same hotel and they might get together for breakfast. During those times, you seldom — or never — heard them talk about the Lord. They talked about the business, the industry, and funny things that happened.

At times, we appeared at fairs. A couple of times we were on the Grand Old Gospel portion of the Grand Old Opry. I felt out of place in some of those situations. It seemed as if we were casting pearls before swine. I wondered why promoters would want to put us there.

R.P. — *You left gospel music not knowing if you would ever travel and sing professionally again?*

Janet — That's true. I suppose you could say that after a number of years I just became very tired of traveling. About a year before I left, the Lord began preparing my heart for a change, and I was really looking forward to it when the change finally came. I went to school for a year and a half back in North Carolina before I came here.

R.P. — *Without sounding self-serving to Jimmy Swaggart or this Ministry, can you contrast the difference between what you were doing and now?*

Janet — I had been acquainted with Brother Swaggart's ministry for many years and had attended crusades some years back. But I guess I wasn't prepared for seeing all the hungry, responsive people in the coliseums. Right away, I knew my singing material would have to be more ministry-oriented as opposed to getting people on their feet to clap, or hitting the charts with a song, or pleasing the producers in the studio.

One of the things that so impressed me with Brother Swaggart was that worldly possessions didn't mean anything to him. I had never seen that attribute in anyone before. I had been around people who thought that was your testimony — to have cars and jewelry and things like that.

R.P. — *Did you notice that the music was building towards something — to prepare people's hearts to hear the Word of God?*

Janet — Yes, I did. In particular, I noticed Brother Swaggart would do his songs with a verse, a chorus, and then he'd play a whole instrumental chorus before finishing with another verse. In gospel music, people say you can't hold anybody's attention that long.

When I came here, I found Brother Swaggart singing songs that are fifty years old. He'll do the entire song in that manner, yet it will hold your attention. It might not have chord changes or nifty little runs, but it has the anointing of the Holy Spirit. I realized it didn't take any of those changes. It simply took the anointing.

As I see lives changed, people being saved and filled with the Spirit, I feel the Lord has lifted me to a higher plane. The results — especially in the overseas countries — are just staggering. To realize I have a small part in this is very humbling.

R.P. — *What's the sharpest contrast between this kind of ministry and singing on the gospel circuit?*

Janet — Motivation. In gospel music, your whole reason for being there is the desire to be in a group. Of course, money enters into it as well as other factors. Here, there is a lot of hard work and a lot of pressure, but there is a difference. I believe the reason everybody is here is because the Lord sent them. I realize this is an opportunity from the Lord and I need to make the best of it. The possibilities of reaching millions of people all over the world are just staggering.

R.P. — *I'm sure you know some of the horror stories about the personal lives of people in gospel music — and we really haven't talked about that specifically. However, if you could change the gospel music circuit in any way, knowing what you know today, what changes would you make?*

Janet — I would probably eliminate about three-fourths of the people now singing gospel music. That would leave the sincere ones, the cream of the crop. I know some people are there because of family, or they like the spotlight and autograph seekers, or they simply want to travel. In particular, I would eliminate those who have no relationship with the Lord.

R.P. — *I know you still have friends in gospel music. If you could directly speak to them about their lives and the industry, what would you tell them?*

Janet — I'd say something like this: I appreciate what you are doing. I can appreciate your love for gospel music, for I too have felt that same zeal. I would like to challenge you to minister more effectively than perhaps you have ever done before. My challenge is to make Jesus Christ the Lord of your music. Ask the Holy Spirit to direct your decision-making, your arrangements, your programs, your bookings — every facet of your music ministry.

Then your music will begin to touch the hearts of more people than ever before, for the Holy Spirit knows the hearts of the people to whom you sing. He can penetrate the heart, bless and uplift, convict and direct lives.

I challenge you to pray for the anointing of the Holy Spirit over every service, every performance, and every decision in your ministry. I challenge you to check your priorities and examine your motives, your attitudes — even your hearts — and say with David:

> *"Search me, O God, and know my heart: try me, and know my thoughts:*
> *"And see if there be any wicked way in me, and lead me in the way everlasting"* (Psa. 139:23, 24).

WHAT TO LOOK FOR IN CHRISTIAN MUSIC?

t seems most Christian artists are not students of the Word of God. They are students of how to have hit records, how to get the best publishing deal, but they are not also students of the Word of God, which has got to be central to all that.

— A producer/agent in *What About Christian Rock?*

Taste will always vary in musical expressions.

And with that thought in mind, no one should ever attempt to project his or her tastes as uniquely pleasing to God. For instance, I shouldn't automatically assume my preference is the only suitable type for the whole spectrum of Christianity.

Yet I have been accused of that very thing. In fact, *Newsweek* magazine quoted a musician who said: "He [Swaggart] is saying, 'Burn all your other albums and buy mine.'"

Nothing could be further from the truth!

However, I believe there must be a *standard* — defined by the Holy Spirit — as to what is correct and proper musical expression within the gospel realm.

Personally, I feel that every singer, performer, artist, and musician who names the name of Jesus Christ must ask himself repeatedly, "Is this the direction the Lord wants for me? Is this the type of music the Lord wants played? Can the Holy Spirit bless this music? Can He anoint it?"

This approach is not something that can be done once and set aside. It involves a continuing process. Why? Because it is very easy to cross over from that which is pleasing to God into an area which is *not* pleasing to Him.

Many times in playing a song I have sensed the Holy Spirit leading me to change the type "fills" I might be using. Perhaps they were not compatible with His way. Even though it might have excited the crowd, I sensed it was not what He wanted.

Countless times I have changed an arrangement that our band had put together for the Jimmy Swaggart Telecast — simply because I felt it did not minister as it was designed to do. Thus, it *had* to be changed.

Scripture exhorts us to fill our minds with:

". . . *whatsoever things are true, whatsoever things are honest, whatsoever things are just, whatsoever things are pure, whatsoever things are lovely, whatsoever things are of good report"* (Phil. 4:8).

With all of this in mind, I offer the following five suggestions, under the guidance of the Holy Spirit, in considering your musical listening interests. The material was adapted from a series of messages preached by Glen Berteau, Youth Pastor at Family Worship Center in Baton Rouge.

(1) *Do you listen to records where the music outweighs the message?*

If that happens, the Holy Spirit is grieved. A good message can make it without good music. In fact, a good message does not even need *any* music.

A crossover message must have the high-tech sound in order to make it appealing. Why? Because such music dilutes its power to have an impact on people's lives and thus technology has to be employed to make up the difference.

A good percentage of the new religious rock desires to use fewer references to Jesus and focus more on issues. Changed lives aren't produced by such music.

Changed lives are produced through the singing of the Word. *"That he might sanctify and cleanse it with the washing of water by the word"* (Eph. 5:26).

The Word actually has a cleansing effect on our lives. Music as such cannot produce that. If you remove the cleansing agent from the song, then you remove any cleaning which can be accomplished.

If a person is physically dirty, he needs a softening agent applied. That's the purpose of water in cleaning. It's difficult — almost impossible — to get physically clean without water. The same is true in the spiritual sense: a person needs the Word to get cleaned up. It's God's cleansing agent.

The more this cleansing agent is removed from religious songs, the less effect will be experienced by those hearing the music. That's an obvious conclusion.

Many religious rock concerts could be called "mud-and-water events." It's a mixture of a little Scripture about Jesus (the Word) but a lot of the world (the mud). A person can't get clean in such a mixture. People may leave the concert partially clean but still spotted by the grime.

That's not God's highest and best for His people. A pure, unadulterated message on the Lord Jesus Christ must be declared.

(2) *Do you listen to groups whose methods (or stage productions) outweigh their message?*

When attending a concert, a person needs to ask some questions: Does a performer's manner of dress and appearance have more of an impact than his music or message? How about the trappings around the stage — the lights, the smoke devices, the strobe lights, the sound machines — Do they make more impact than the message?

The secular rockers all have a gimmick. It might be a new digital sound system, a tremendous light show, a special effects smoke machine, or a host of other considerations. Yet each *relies* on a gimmick.

The ruse could be the onstage antics of W.A.S.P., of Ozzy Osbourne tossing pieces of raw animal flesh to the howling crowd. Or it could be the outrageous costumes and makeup of Motley Crue. The group KISS wore heavy black and white facial makeup for years and then scored a "publicity coup" when the band unmasked from the paint to reveal their faces to an adoring public.

It's always a stunt!

The world will always use methods or gimmicks because that's the characteristic nature of the devil. He always tries to outdo himself. The more atrocious the stunt becomes, usually the more impressed people are — especially naive young people.

Larry Tomczak suggested in an article on "Today's Music" in *Destiny* magazine:

> Let's face it squarely: Worldly performance tactics have absolutely no place in Christian music! While our Lord wants us to enjoy life and music to the fullest (John 10:10) — at times even "leaping for joy" (Luke 6:23) and "crying out" from our innermost being as He Himself did (John 7:37) — there are some areas we need to avoid. By no means exhaustive, these are some areas that should be obvious to us all:
>
> • Deliberately sensual, breathy voice and erotic movements designed to arouse an audience.
>
> • Provocative and/or revealing clothes that are not in line with biblical modesty.
>
> • Unedifying speech: put-downs, suggestive jokes, stories with double meanings (the second being immoral), sexual overtones, sarcasm, and satire that cross the boundaries of decency and grace.
>
> • Blaring, thunderous decibel levels that consistently and totally drown out lyrics — *"If the trumpet does not sound a clear call, who will get ready for battle? So it is with you. Unless you speak intelligible words with your tongue, how will anyone know what you are saying?"* (I Cor. 14:8, 9).
>
> • Flirtatious come-ons designed to titillate and sexually tease onlookers.
>
> • Violent destruction of property — guitars, amplifiers, and other expensive equipment. Even if this is intended to be a statement of rejecting materialism, most impressionable young people won't know this and too often tend to emulate the behavior of those they admire.

(3) Discernment of album covers.

I am not suggesting here that every Christian performer wear a glowing white suit and a gold-trimmed halo. However, I am suggesting if your favorite performer is imitating the world on his album cover, that's a reflection of a decline right there.

Have you seen the recent photographs on some album covers? These pictures of angry young men sporting punk and new wave clothing certainly seem to convey nothing about "the joy of the Lord" which is supposed to be our strength.

If you place some of the religious rockers' albums side-by-side with secular rock artists, there is very little difference in appearance or presentation — to say nothing about the similarity in musical styles.

What About Christian Rock? quotes Prodigal's Loyd Boldman as saying:

> I think it's way past the time when we ought to be imitating the world as far as how we do things . . . A lot of people nowadays — especially Christians — wait until some new pop thing happens and everyone jumps on it. Suddenly there's half a dozen Amy Grants or Michael McDonalds or Kenny Loggins sound-alikes. It's pretty much the same thing with looks. Take heavy metal. All of a sudden Christian bands are finding out, "Oh! Heavy metal for the Lord! Let's all go rip our shirts and wear chains!"

It seems to me if an artist is growing in the grace and knowledge of the Lord Jesus, that growth would also be reflected in the person's musical direction. Many albums reflect more of the world than they do Christ.

The direction of many of the religious rockers is not towards the Lord Jesus but simply to emulate successful trends, patterns, and styles of the world in dress and musical sound. At times "bizarreness masquerades as creativity" and for some reason the religious rock artists fall right in line with the world.

Don't buy a crossover album. No such music will ever be heard in heaven. There won't be anything resembling it in the Eternal City. Don't waste your time with it here on earth. It has no value in the Kingdom of God.

> *"Ye adulterers and adulteresses, know ye not that the friendship of the world is enmity with God? whosoever therefore will be a friend of the world is the enemy of God"* (James 4:4).

(4) *Character of the artist.*

Do you sense the anointing of the Holy Spirit upon that singer or musician or the group as a whole? Does the person's ministry and life bear genuine fruit and does that fruit remain? Does that person live a life worthy of being followed?

A veteran music producer/agent has been quoted as saying:

> Other things are more important than what happens on our stages — it's what happens in real life. We in the Christian music industry are so cutesy in explaining away the absolutes of the Gospel . . . And we think we can have a wonderful ministry. I say that's nonsense.

When I read about the musical inspiration for many of the religious rockers and hear the public statements they've made, I seriously question the personal integrity of many of these artists.

Moreover, I'm very concerned about this pattern of attempting to bridge the gap between Christian and pop music. I wonder about the motives of artists in making such an appeal — especially in light of the fact that there appears to be no genuine fruit of all the efforts expended.

Yet it seems that a large percentage of the religious rockers appear headed in the direction of twin careers — one in the religious arena and a second in the secular.

Retired military personnel, still on the government payroll in civil service work, are often characterized as "double-dipping" from the government treasury. Much of religious rock seems headed for twin paychecks as well. Is the motive simply money?

Are these religious rockers a viable part of a local church? By looking at many of their traveling schedules, it's obvious many are on the road for weeks — and even months — at a time. What then happens to their spiritual life?

The local church, according to the Word of God, is supposed to be the vehicle for training and discipleship. It is imperative that any musician or gospel singer be established in a strong, Bible-believing, local church. This is the place where accountability is established.

Religious rockers, not committed in a New Testament church, are in reality "spiritual Lone Rangers" headed for big-time trouble. Without that church connection, it is virtually impossible for any individual to be taught, nurtured, and even admonished in the things of the Lord.

By following the biblical pattern of church membership (I Cor. 12:18) and laboring under proper pastoral authority (Heb. 13:17), a person establishes his credibility to preach or sing about the Lord Jesus Christ.

Without such credibility, a person — in all honesty — really has no right at all to minister for it is a clear breach of Scripture.

(5) *Does the music stir the flesh to "boogie" or to praise the Lord?*

Another question could be asked as well: Does the music enhance the spiritual nature or the carnal nature of your life?

When several young people in Baton Rouge attended the Stryper concert, they were asked by Youth Pastor Glen Berteau, "What did that music make you want to do?"

Both of the young men in question, who were relatively new converts, agreed that the music was bad for them. One teenager said, *"It gives me a flashback and makes me want to go out and do dope again."*

The other agreed there was a negative inspiration to the music. "It makes me want to go home, get my electric guitar, and play the heaviest rock and roll I can," he admitted.

These teenagers' comments, as well as considerable documented material, have convinced me of the falseness of the religious rock sound. It didn't cause these young people to praise the Lord. They were only inspired in their fleshly nature.

> *"For he that soweth to his flesh shall of the flesh reap corruption; but he that soweth to the Spirit shall of the Spirit reap life everlasting"* (Gal. 6:8).

That in one simple declarative sentence is what religious rock and roll is producing. It's stirring the flesh of young people and producing adherents to a musical sound — not drawing youngsters to the Person of the Lord Jesus Christ.

Salvation in Christ means you become a new person. You have a renewed mind. You function under the Lordship of Jesus Christ. It means you sing a new song. Old things have passed away and everything has become new (II Cor. 5:17).

> *"And be renewed in the spirit of your mind;*
> *"And that ye put on the new man, which after*
> *God is created in righteousness and true holi-*
> *ness"* (Eph. 4:23, 24).

That's what *genuine* salvation is all about!

It doesn't "retread" the mores, methods, and music of the world and try to hang a Christian label on it. God doesn't need that. Jesus is simply all we need.

CHAPTER FOURTEEN

WHO OR WHAT'S TO BLAME?

 hese kids are not simply memorizing our lyrics. They're living their lives by what we're telling them in our songs, and that has big consequences!
— Religious Rocker in *CCM* Magazine

A popular youth evangelist recently told me about a large meeting in a metropolitan city in Canada where he preached to some 7,000 young people. The music for the gathering was provided by one of the top male singers in religious rock and his band.

The program began with the musical group at 8 o'clock and the youth evangelist was scheduled to begin preaching at 9 p.m. Instead, the singer and his band took a *full* hour and 50 minutes.

It was almost 10 o'clock before the youth evangelist was introduced to preach. The scene before him defied almost anything he'd previously seen in ministry.

Seven thousand young people were shouting, screaming, and clapping. Many had been dancing in the aisles and milling around the auditorium while the singer had taken the extra 50 minutes. The last song the musical group performed had — in the evangelist's words — "put the kids on the ceiling."

It took the young preacher some while to get the teenagers in the audience settled. Several times he was forced to yell, "Please sit down . . . be quiet."

Finally, the audience calmed from its musical frenzy and the youth evangelist preached a tremendous message under the anointing of the Holy Spirit. Hundreds of young people — many of them broken and weeping — streamed forward.

Before he had stepped to the microphone to preach, the preacher had asked the coordinator in charge of the meeting to have the band ready to play at the altar call. In fact, he had requested a special song which exactly fit his message.

Now he looked around anxiously for the singer and his band. The musical group never showed back up. Under great pressure with several hundred teenagers at the altar, the young preacher finished the service.

He walked backstage afterwards and asked the coordinator, "What happened? Where was the band?"

"The singer didn't want to come out," the man responded. "He felt that wasn't in his contract."

"His contract?" the youth evangelist mumbled.

The next day the young preacher was given a check for $700 for his services. He thanked the minister in charge of the gathering and asked, "How does this compare with the fee the band received?"

"Oh, that was $6,500," came the reply.

The young preacher was shocked — as I was — at the value placed on the music over the value placed on God's messenger. It didn't make sense. The music had done nothing but stir the flesh of the thousands in attendance.

It was only through the preaching of the Word of God that any lasting results came from the meeting. Yet the priority had been placed on the music.

Unfortunately, I am convinced this story is repeated countless times across the Body of Christ.

Why does such a situation currently exist? What can really be done about such misplaced priorities? Here are some issues and answers which have been drawn from a series of messages preached by Glen Berteau, Youth Pastor at Family Worship Center:

(1) *Why do churches and youth pastors book these religious rock groups in the first place?*

There is significant pressure from pastors to have a crowd. I know of churches where the number one objective is to have a lot of people in attendance. To a youth worker, that might justify his position in the church, or even make him feel important if an event can be promoted with a large crowd.

Unfortunately, big crowds don't necessarily mean a concert is of God. Further, just because a popular group with a hit album performs and thousands attend doesn't make it a Godly event.

In truth, such concerts are often a simple reflection of the spiritual depth of the people in attendance. As well, they are also a reflection of the youth pastor's spirituality.

Some pastors will allow these kinds of concerts sponsored by their churches because they simply don't know. There is little teaching about religious rock. Thus, understanding on the subject tends to be very limited.

That's one of the basic reasons for this book — to provide crucial information to the Body of Christ so that a Spirit-led conclusion can be reached on religious rock by God's people.

Another factor is that larger churches *intimidate* smaller churches, while small churches *imitate* larger churches.

A smaller church will ride in a piggy-back fashion on the program of a larger church body. If a larger church is having concerts and musical programs with religious rock artists, then a small church will do the same. It becomes acceptable in a smaller church because a larger congregation has done it first.

Where in the Bible does it state this is the criterion for making such decisions? That kind of approach is in the same league with the "comparison tests" comparing secular rock artists and religious rockers. All such approaches have no biblical foundation.

Each of us must simply stick with the Bible in our decision-making efforts. That is the only means I know of to keep God's people from getting their ox carts stuck in the ditch.

> *"And he spake a parable unto them, Can the blind lead the blind? shall they not both fall into the ditch?"* (Luke 6:39).

(2) *Are these religious rockers producing the very results churches are bringing them into town for?*

If the concerts are staged in coliseums or city auditoriums and young people actually step forward to receive Christ, where will they go to church? Who will do the routine follow-up necessary to bring them into mature discipleship?

If the concert is held in a particular church, will it produce converts to Jesus who will be active, ongoing members of the congregation?

All of these are valid considerations when evaluating the proof of a person's ministry — although I know many of the religious rockers' disdain at the use of the word "ministry." However, the validity of anyone's efforts — whether in evangelism or religious rock — is *results*.

Ironically, many of the so-called crossover artists talk about results that are not tangible.

I am speaking of *genuine* conversions, not just those who have been *"blessed by the positive, moral message."* I'm talking about a wholesale surrender of a person's life to the Lordship of Christ, repenting of the old life and beginning a new life characterized by righteousness, peace, and joy in the Holy Ghost. Nothing else can truly signify the born-again experience.

If young people were really coming to Jesus — in the manner in which some of the religious rockers claim — there wouldn't be room enough to hold them in the churches. There would be massive church construction everywhere to accommodate the numbers.

I've heard thousands are being saved. In one recent interview, one religious rocker stated, ". . . 100,000 people have accepted Christ."

If that's the case, I simply ask, "Where are they?"

Also, the standard for having a religious rock group in a church is significantly different than having a visiting evangelist. That guest preacher will have cleared some major hurdles before the local pastor allows him to grace the church pulpit.

For instance, the pastor will know something about the preacher's personal life, his testimony, and about his relationship to a local church. He may even call other churches where the evangelist has preached to check out his efforts. Then there are the questions about doctrine and denominational affiliation — which can all be thorny issues. All in all, it can be an exhaustive effort before the visiting preacher ever stands to speak.

That's hardly the case with a singer or a musical group. If they have an album being played over the radio or a video on television or have appeared as guests on one of the popular TV talk shows, they are *automatically qualified.*

Their personal life may be in shambles. The band members may have all backslidden and have no ongoing relationship with Christ, but they will have a ready, responsive full house when they come to "perform."

And, sadly, few people will ever know the difference.

A youth pastor at a large southern California church examined that problem in the Winter 86-87 *Calendar* magazine:

> . . . Times have changed and contemporary music ministries are springing up left and right . . . With this, I'm afraid, has come less accountability and less oversight. This is one reason we see ministries falling away, slipping into heresies, etc.
>
> I must admit, I've been burned by just such ministries, some of which are well known. The artist or band arrived in town only to be spiritually arrogant, theologically unsound, or with a marriage relationship in sin. As I pushed for information with these groups, I found in *every* case no home church and no pastoral oversight.
>
> Many of the above-mentioned ministries have ended abruptly due to member disputes, outright sin, or perhaps a lack of bookings. I've since become more selective in choosing the ministry which I want to represent our Lord on my church stage. Some of the criteria for selection reads like this: "Are you regularly attending church? Where? Is the Pastor aware of the ministry and does he support it?"

In closing the article, the youth pastor made a strong observation about the religious rockers' connection to a local church:

. . . Little is said about the local church from your
stages because *few of you attend.* (Italics mine.)

(3) *This question is directed to church leadership: Are your young people becoming more holy and closer to Jesus because of listening to religious rock?*

If a person is utilizing religious rock for his growth and maturity instead of time spent in the Bible and in prayer, that individual is on a spiritual crash course. It's just a matter of time before the collision occurs. You can practically set your watch in preparation for the disaster.

There is no power and no spiritually sustaining strength from religious rock. It wouldn't surprise me at all if that person walked away from God over a period of time.

A young person can dance in the aisles, rush the stage of their favorite performer and shout "fight on" while shaking a fist in the devil's face — but there is no enriching, edifying, or upbuilding of the Spirit man in his heart. There is simply nothing to feed the Spirit from religious rock. It's like eating a frothy cotton candy which has no substance.

The power to overcome the devil has to be in your heart, not in your ear! It has to be down deep in the inner person, and that can only be developed by communion with God through reading His Word, concentrated prayer, and sitting under anointed preaching. It is further developed through intimate times of praise and worship with God, and utilizing the gift of the Holy Ghost.

If a young person's life reflects the styles in dress, in music, and in conversation as those expressed by the religious rockers, there can be no genuine fruit of the Spirit produced. *It is only a paltry reflection of the world.* It represents none of the character and spirit of the Lord Jesus.

To our pastors and youth workers, I encourage you to look at your young people and see what this brand of music is producing in them. Is it fruit of this world? Or fruit of the blessed Holy Spirit? The latter is from God; the former is not.

Your responsibility as a leader is to develop the quality and character of the Lord Jesus in your people. If that is not happening, you need to seek the face of God until it does occur. For surely the Holy Spirit would be satisfied with nothing less in all of God's people.

(4) *Who is to blame for the role currently being played by the religious rockers in the Body of Christ?*

That blame or responsibility rests squarely on the shoulders of leadership in the church, and both pastors and youth pastors are culpable in these areas.

If individual churches and denominational groups stopped booking these musical groups, that would make a drastic difference in religious rock's impact. Interestingly, it's not just a few denominations involved; the list could cover the Body of Christ: Assemblies of God, Baptist, Church of God, Lutheran, Methodist, Presbyterian, Foursquare, Word of Faith, and independents from one end of the spectrum to the other, as well as a host of church-related colleges.

Further, if Christian bookstores would quit stocking the individuals' records, tapes, and videos, that would be another great step in the right direction.

Lastly, if gospel radio stations would establish some standards for records played, that would severely limit the airtime of religious rock since most of that music would get the axe.

What would be the result of such drastic steps? I honestly believe only the God-called groups would remain. Mylon LeFevre surprisingly has been quoted in *Destiny* magazine with making a similar comment:

> If money wasn't being made, there wouldn't be many people doing it. It would be wonderful if there wasn't any money being made for the next year, the only people left would be the people that love Jesus. . . .

I'm sure there are those in religious rock, like Mylon and others, who genuinely love the Lord. Yet loving Jesus has nothing to do with being part of a musical trend — religious rock — which is adversely affecting the church of Jesus Christ. It's a case of terribly "wrong direction" on the part of the religious rockers.

None of these people would be playing religious rock if money was not being made. Money is the name of the game.

I'm reminded of a phone call my office received from a beer company after I preached a hard message over television on the evils of drinking. The caller attempted to convince my secretary his company was one of the "good beer distributors."

As far as I'm concerned, that company is *worse* than the rest in attempting to place a false facade over what the beer industry creates. Yet it shows you how reasonably intelligent people can be fooled.

The same is true in religious rock. Individuals may continue playing the music and still maintain some type of consecration in their life, but they are only fooling themselves. They are part and parcel of the whole problem.

At times, I am sure that some in church leadership, as well as bookstore owners and radio stations, might offer this religious rock out of ignorance. I find that difficult to understand, but giving everyone the benefit of a doubt, it is possible.

However, I could not understand anyone still providing a conduit of religious rock to their congregation, radio audience, or bookstore customers after reading the information contained in this book. An individual would have to

172 Religious Rock and Roll

override what the Holy Spirit has imparted to continue as a channel of this religious rock and roll.

Then, the bottom line becomes the grossest reason of all — covetness. In other words, the dollar bill.

**CHAPTER
FIFTEEN**

CROSSFIRE:
AN ALTERNATIVE

*he church should be the salt of the earth. We should
have a new song and new music. Why would we want to
baptize a form of music that is born, bred, and raised in
sin? Why should we put our message in old wine sacks?*
— David Noebel

The book, *The Heart of Rock and Roll,* closed its
profile of singer Steve Taylor with the following comment:

A Christian rocker/humorist/satirist as an example for
American youth?
Would you prefer Twisted Sister?

That's the proposal that religious rock continues to
offer: our brand of rock and roll or the world's.

I say *neither* will do. I consider both to be in gross error.

The church does not have to accept this mistaken
proposition of "either/or," for I believe the end results to

secular rock and religious rock will be the same — spiritual wreckage. There is another way — an alternative.

Perhaps you were already asking that question. Maybe you were even wondering if I had any concrete suggestions for reaching young people at all. Needless to say, I do, and that approach has nothing to do with the use of religious rock.

Through our church in Baton Rouge, Family Worship Center, now some 6,000 strong, I have witnessed the development of a superb program based on the Word of God for reaching the youth. This book's co-author, Robert Paul Lamb, conducted the following interview with Glen Berteau, Youth Pastor, on the Crossfire ministry.

R.P.: *What is the Crossfire ministry?*

Glen: It's a youth ministry based on two elements — spirit and truth. That means praise and worship, along with the preaching of the Word of God, are the bottom line in everything we do.

R.P.: *How did it get started here in Baton Rouge?*

Glen: We began about two years ago with 40 typical church youth. The first thing I wanted to teach them was how to praise and worship. They were taught it's not a Pentecostal or Assemblies of God doctrine for lifting your hands and clapping. I taught them what the Word of God says.

I also preached sermons on commitment to the Lord. If you are meeting the needs of youth, they won't be concerned with playing volleyball and a host of other activities (although we have activities). They will want to hear what will fill the void in their lives. Young people don't think much ahead so I dealt with meeting their most pressing needs, such as how can I function in school tomorrow, why should I live for God, why should I be radical, why should I be on the offensive?

In the first place, young people are very militant, but too often we don't give them anything to fight for. The church caters to their wants and desires — which are game-oriented and sugar-coated meetings. This never has and it never will help a young person stand for God in this generation.

R.P.: *Once you got the 40 committed to the Lord, what was your next step?*

Glen: At that point, many of them began bringing their friends because our efforts were evangelistic. Shortly, the group doubled to about 80 and we began home fellowship groups. Our purposes for these groups are praise and worship, prayer, and Bible study. We learned that a lot of things can occur in a small group setting that can't take place in the main meeting. You can't disciple from the pulpit. That is done in a separate meeting.

R.P.: *What are the ages of the people involved?*

Glen: From 12 to 22. Now you'll have a problem with youth pastors thinking that can't be done, but all they have to do is come here and see the proof.

Many would ask, "How do you put the 12-year-old in with the 22-year-old?" It's simple. They walk in and we preach to them. We don't have junior high sermons and adult sermons; we just preach the Word of God. You don't just throw around little slang words trying to be trendy. You communicate God's Word.

The Bible says the older should help the younger and that's what we've found in this ministry. The older kids help the junior highers to bring their Bibles, notepads, and pens.

R.P.: *Do you insist on that when the group comes? The Bibles, notepads, and pens?*

Glen: Yes, we do. We've also found the junior high youth will not act up because they see the older, more mature people worshiping and praising God. They don't want to be considered childish so that helps a great deal. And just like everybody else, the junior high youth get their needs met in the fellowship groups. These groups are divided into three age brackets — junior high, high school, and young adults.

R.P.: *Actually, you have more than just the auditorium meeting on Wednesday night?*

Glen: Yes. The main meeting is on Wednesday night but we have our home groups meeting all over the city on Tuesday and Friday nights. We have kept the home groups small in size and that keeps them strong in power.

R.P.: *Are they set up geographically?*

Glen: Yes, but they are based more on location to a particular school area than, say, proximity to Family Worship Center. As I said, we have split and expanded the groups frequently, keeping the number small in the individual homes. In just two years, we have now reached the point where 500 young people are now being discipled each week through the home meetings and our Wednesday night attendance is around 1,000.

R.P.: *Is your approach a new concept or have you employed it elsewhere?*

Glen: We had fellowship groups at Calvary Assembly in Winter Park, Florida, before I came here, but the concept of fellowship groups is used by a lot of different churches. Most people who work with this approach have learned their leadership grows out of the fellowship groups. We have observed also that many of the youth grow stronger in the Lord as a result of the home fellowships.

R.P.: *Okay, your program has then developed in two ways. What was the next logical step?*

Glen: From our home meetings, we have also begun Crossfire Clubs around the city. Many of the strong Christians developed in the meetings at home go to their schools and meet as a campus club.

We also began a visitation program. The young people contact 800 or more people each week. We use the phone, personal visits, letters. We also have a bus ministry. Youth who cannot get rides are bussed from various parts of the city. It's an intricate network where each part complements the other but the centerpiece is the Wednesday night meeting.

R.P.: *So in reality, there are a number of opportunities for the youth during the week?*

Glen: Right. We have the Wednesday night meeting, then the home fellowships on Tuesday and Friday. During the week, there is a campus club meeting at school. We have these in seven or eight public high schools at present. On Saturday morning, we have visitation. Presently we have about 80 to 90 young people out for that. Also, many of the youth will come in Tuesday night to make phone calls as a part of visitation. Then, of course, there is church on Sunday.

R.P.: *Well, the results you've seen here surely indicate something is working with young people.*

Glen: That's right. We now have about 1,000 young people here every Wednesday night.

R.P.: *Did you ever try booking religious rock bands to help with your efforts?*

Glen: Before the musical trend had reached the level it has now, I brought in some contemporary groups at my former church. I found the attendance was lower two weeks after the group came. We had expected the groups to bring people into the place but the *actual* result was we had less.

R.P.: *What factor caused that to happen?*

Glen: I don't know other than God was not blessing it. I had been told you could bring in these groups, pack out the building, and introduce young people to the church. They would get saved and come back. Unfortunately, that does not happen.

People will argue that point. However, over a four-year period of time, I didn't see our group grow by using that method. In fact, I brought in a well-known religious rock group. We spent several thousand dollars in advertising on a secular rock radio station attempting to reach the unsaved. The concert resulted in a financial loss of about $1,500 and we found the unsaved didn't come anyway.

R.P.: *Who came to that concert?*

Glen: Mostly church youth. I found it was a waste of time and money. It was terrible. Oftentimes, people will push a concert like this as a means of evangelism, but I have found it to be nothing more than a great waste.

People's lives are changed when they see others allowing the love of God to come through and not be intimidated on campus. That's what others are looking for. You have people bragging on campus about how much they drink, how many drugs they take, or who they have slept with. Yet Christian young people will never share the love of God with anybody. They just shut their mouths.

R.P.: *How do you teach young people to overcome this barrier?*

Glen: One thing that leadership must do is guide and show the way. I'll preach a message, for instance, on reaching out to others, and the next week I'm on their campus saying, "Who is your tough guy?" I'll confront that guy who is supposed to be so bad.

What happens is that young people eventually see they can stand for the Lord wherever they are. So I don't just preach messages and ask young people to do these things without me doing them myself. If I can't do what I preach, then I shouldn't preach it. We really have to be radicals for Jesus.

R.P.: *I noticed your youth group wears those T-shirts. What does being a radical for Jesus mean?*

Glen: Actually, it's being normal. You have to use the term radical because we are so far off from the Book of Acts. When we look at the people being radical in the world, it's mostly young people. Beirut is a prime example.

Yet in America we've never given youth anything to fight for. The rock stars have reached the youth by showing them not to take anything from anybody. They've become the leaders of our youth, not because they're so great, but because the average preacher is so weak.

So when a message is preached, it must be acted out or lived out in the life of the person. If that doesn't happen, then all I'm doing is preaching cute little messages and expecting youth to catch this unbelievable vision and just do the work themselves.

R.P.: *The obvious connection is with the Lord Jesus and His followers. No doubt, that's what transformed them. They saw Him in action. So, when Peter and John saw the lame man at the Temple, they did what Jesus would have done — they reached out to him.*

Glen: Exactly. They just didn't hear Him preaching little sermons. They saw Him living what He preached.

R.P.: *Has this ministry approach been successful elsewhere?*

Glen: Yes, we had a youth pastors conference last year with several thousand in attendance. We've received numerous letters from youth pastors whose groups have doubled, or even tripled in size. One group in Canada went from 20 to 100 young people in eight weeks. They came here and saw what we are doing.

I've received letters from youth pastors who said they apologized to their young people for preaching "milk toast" messages. God is honoring youth pastors who will stand up and preach holiness.

R.P.: *Has it been suggested to you that religious rock is the only thing that will help build a youth group?*

Glen: Sure it has. A lot of Christian artists have said if we don't use them, we'll never have a crowd. Jesus said if we would lift Him up, He would draw all men. I think God wants to see if we are going to rely on Him, or if we feel the

Holy Spirit needs help. We don't need the world's system to pack out our youth halls.

R.P.: *So, this approach to ministry can't be limited to a specific geographical area?*

Glen: Not at all. Last year we had young people who went to Kenya and they had kids there asking them about drug problems and sex. Our American youth were shocked. They were the same kind of questions youth from the states face every day. It is universal because sin is universal.

R.P.: *What's the mistaken fallacy behind the suggestion you must use this heavy rock sound to reach young people?*

Glen: Well, if you're into getting a crowd, you can get a crowd through that method. However, if you're into *keeping* a crowd, it won't keep them. So the question comes down to getting or keeping a crowd. What are you after?

I know our approach sounds too simple to work, but that's because most have gotten so far away from preaching the Bible. And certainly we don't preach enough on the character of the inner person. The Bible says where the Lord is, there is life, liberty, and the anointing. If those three are not present in a meeting, the Spirit of God may not be there.

R.P.: *How would you answer the person who says your approach is working because you're a dynamic individual, or this is Jimmy Swaggart's home church? They might even suggest that Baton Rouge is a little easier than their town might be.*

Glen: Baton Rouge would be harder than most cities because the majority of people here are Catholics (actually, I was raised Catholic myself). Jimmy Swaggart is one of the most influential men in the city. However, there are many people here who are strongly opposed to his ministry because of his stand for the Word of God.

R.P.: *How would you respond to the youth pastor who says you don't understand how hard his town is to reach with the Gospel?*

Glen: That's a cop-out. I've heard the same thing when people say they can't get on school campuses. That's a thought of failure. It suggests God is not big enough for the situation.

I'd say that person does not understand God. Isn't God bigger than that? Don't you think God can knock down the walls of that situation? It's ridiculous to think of all the reasons we seemingly can't accomplish anything. I've heard people say, "I've tried and tried and tried." Well, they should keep trying; maybe next time they will overcome. They will not continue to lose if they keep going on with God. They will eventually find the way.

R.P.: *I read the other day about a full-gospel church which is using contemporary music in its youth group. They have a tape-lending library and they spend time discussing the song lyrics. What would you suggest to them about their activites?*

Glen: I'd say most of religious rock's lyrics are very shallow. The songs have little meat of the Word of God. Most of the lyrics are not strong enough to help anybody stand up for the Lord for any consistent length of time. The Bible says if you are on the milk of the Word, you are unskillful in the use of the Word. Leonard Ravenhill said that 95 percent of all so-called Christians are babies or carnal. He said that's like finding out your Army, Navy, Air Force, and Marines are manned by Cub Scouts.

R.P.: *Do you regard it as a totally mistaken notion to suggest that religious rock is necessary to attract young people?*

Glen: It is not needed. The only way we use music in our program is for praise and worship. That is the only kind of music we utilize. Get your young people to love God, and they won't need a lot of music. A lot of the religious rock is going to stir their flesh anyway. It is going to stir a lot of emotions that will not attract them to fall in love with God.

Is music a part of a young person's life? I'd say very much so. But they are going to operate on what their leaders are saying. There are a lot of people willing to die for a cause but most of them are not Christians. Yet we all seem to want to use supplements. Religious rock is nothing more than a supplement, a generic religious supplement. It is a substitute for the real thing. It is not authentic.

I can honestly say in 11 to 12 years of youth ministry I have never seen religious rock cause young people to grow or be strengthened in the Lord. And I can further say, I have never seen it contribute to the building of any youth ministry I have been associated with.

Now understand, you've got some Godly singers out there who can come in, sing, and bless people. However, I have discovered many of the groups are tearing down what I'm trying to do with the youth. I simply ask, are we saving the lost or losing the "found"?

R.P.: *Why do you think they are tearing down?*

Glen: Because they are using the world's standards and the world's music, thinking it will attract people. I haven't honestly seen any tangible fruits of what these people say they are accomplishing.

If you look at religious rock from the standpoint of packing an auditorium, it will work. Some will talk about the light show and the musical talents of the musicians. You'll hear those comments all the time. But as far as providing people with becoming closer to God, they are very shallow and do not deal anywhere in the area of maturing people in the Lord.

R.P.: *You preached a strong series of messages on religious rock. What was the net effect of that effort among your young people?*

Glen: First of all, I must say, that series was preached only after two years of strong foundational groundwork for this ministry. I could not have preached such a series unless these young people had seen me as a man of God. They would have probably walked out otherwise.

I prayed for special wisdom and guidance before delivering the messages and took four weeks in presenting the material. The youth flooded in to hear the messages because there is so little available on the subject. I didn't give my opinions; I basically quoted other individuals — much as you have done in this book.

I had young people tell me they wanted to live for God and they threw away tapes from most of the singers and groups I had named. That was an immediate reaction.

We are raising young people to the point of understanding that any kind of sin is wrong. Holiness is the key word of the day. Power and anointing are available to these young people. We'll see great results because of God's character working in their lives.

Young people who don't have this character in their lives will have difficulty in seeing this message. Holiness and purity are basically foreign words to them.

Yet I have found young people are saying, "Give me something to stand for, give me something to fight for." Oftentimes the young people are caught in the middle of two opposing viewpoints. They're tired of that spot. But, of course, the real problem is the leadership.

R.P.: *How do you see that problem being solved?*

Glen: It's done by each individual personally checking out his own life. I've got to see where I'm weak and then work at developing my potential in the Lord. When God opens me up one day like a frog in a laboratory and looks at my inner motives, what is He going to see? Did I dress in the trendy fashions of the day and wear the hairstyle of the rock stars? People aren't coming to Christ because of that. Lost people could care less.

R.P.: *I understand that you had a personal meeting with Stryper some months ago. How would you describe that conversation?*

Glen: That's right. I attended their Baton Rouge concert at their invitation and then went backstage to talk to them. I spoke with them about the Lord inhabiting the praises of His people. I asked if they felt they had praised the Lord that night? The answer was "yes." I also asked if they felt they had an anointing? Again, the answer was "yes." Robert Sweet told me that when he's not playing his drums, he's off praying because of the demonic forces he continually battles.

I also asked why they didn't give an altar call. They said there were two reasons: Jesus gives silent altar calls, meaning that you don't have to do anything. He knocks at the door. They also said they were afraid if people came forward, they might rip their clothes off.

Robert didn't say it had happened before but I somehow felt it might have been attempted. He also told me that they are the only people reaching out to the heavy metal rock crowd.

R.P.: *In your view, is there any credible evidence to suggest they are reaching anybody?*

Glen: Based on the concert I witnessed, there was not enough Gospel in what they are doing to reach people who do not know the Lord or the mechanics of salvation. I lived twenty years without the Lord at all. I didn't know anything about Jesus.

Looking back, I might have gone to a Stryper concert if they had been around in those days because I played the guitar. However, based on what they are giving out, there would have been no way I could have gotten saved. There's not enough Gospel presented to walk away from their concert knowing anything.

They might be singing about Jesus in a song but as a lost person that would have meant absolutely nothing to me. I would have been more interested in watching the drummer or the other musicians. I might have understood their message if they stopped the music and presented Christ. Stryper did stop the music but they didn't say *anything*.

If an unsaved person goes into one of these concerts, nothing will happen unless he's prepped beforehand on how to get saved.

R.P.: *How did your conversation with Stryper end?*

Glen: It ran for about two to two and a half hours. I told them we are reaching young people at all levels of society — drug addicts, alcoholics, Satan worshipers, and just about anything else — and we're doing it without religious rock. We've chosen to reach young people through God's Word. We don't need the methods of the world's culture . . . and that's a fact.

R.P.: *If Crossfire is that successful, how can it be duplicated elsewhere?*

Glen: It's not just a phenomenon happening in one place. It is an approach that can be duplicated in any city in this country — but only if the vessel carrying the message is unobstructed by the things of the world.

It has become successful because God is doing it. It's authentic because nothing has been added; the ingredients are holy. I don't think God or the Holy Spirit needs help in changing lives. I'm not saying we shouldn't have activities and good times. However, I am saying God is the purest form of ministry there is. Why dilute that? Why should we remove ourselves from that?

The leadership must not rely upon the methods used in the world, thinking Godly results will follow. By doing this, the power of God is reduced in a person's life and ministry. Ecclesiastes 10:10 declares:

> *"If the ax is dull, and one does not sharpen the edge, then he must use more strength, but wisdom brings success"* (NKJV).

AFTERWORD

Young people today are confronting problems I never had to face in my youth. All of the problems of my day are still present but there is also the scourge of drugs, illicit sex, perversion, and Satan worship. But that's just the tip of the iceberg:

• Over half of our young people today are living in broken homes.

• 1,600 a day are attempting suicide, with all too many succeeding.

• The problem of preteen alcoholism is acute.

• Despite rampant abortion, 40,000 teenage girls became pregnant in the U.S. last year. In a disposable society, we now have "throw-away" children. No one wants them.

• Thousands of young people have been sexually molested as a result of the "spirit of the age" fostered by Satan through pornography, Hollywood, and the TV industry.

Does anyone care about these young people? How can they be reached morally and spiritually?

The church does not have to crumble under the onslaught of drugs and perversion. Jesus Christ is equal to the task. The church does have the answer to the problem.

I believe Satan is making his greatest attack against young people today. The master of deceit's time is short and his efforts have grown in intensity and ferocity. He is out to destroy a generation of young people.

Music is not the answer. The Lord Jesus Christ is.

Modern religious rock and roll is not drawing young people to Jesus. It is drawing them to rock concerts. The greatest thing that could happen within the church today would be for all rock musicians to consecrate themselves to God and abandon their obsession with religious rock music.

And what about pastors and church leaders? They should forsake this effort and banish rock music from their churches.

Since rock music invaded the church with its religious lyrics, Satan has been rocking and rolling with laughter. The time has come for the church to end this charade.

If you attend a church where this is being used, go to your pastor and object to these practices. If you are a musician, repent of your ways and ask God to cleanse your heart. If you are a pastor, stand up for righteousness and do God's work.

I pray for you — church members, religious rock musicians, pastors. Above all, I pray that God will open your eyes to the real road His church is traveling.

> *"Behold, I stand at the door, and knock: if any man hear my voice, and open the door, I will come in to him, and will sup with him, and he with me"* (Rev. 3:20).